POLITICS
IN A
MEXICAN COMMUNITY

by *Lawrence S. Graham*

UNIVERSITY OF FLORIDA PRESS / GAINESVILLE, 1968

Para
La Señora Salud G. Viuda de Arce
Nuestra Abuelita Mexicana

ACKNOWLEDGMENTS

For helpful comments and suggestions in the preparation of this monograph I wish to thank Professor Gladys M. Kammerer of the University of Florida and Professors Karl M. Schmitt and Stuart A. MacCorkle of the University of Texas. I am indebted especially to Gladys Kammerer for guidance in becoming familiar with the field of urban politics in the United States, prior to undertaking field work in Mexico. Likewise, I would like to express my appreciation to Stuart MacCorkle, Director of the Institute of Public Affairs at the University of Texas, for a grant received from the Institute during the summer of 1966. This grant was a consequence of the Institute's growing interest in making funds available for research in Latin America. A word of thanks is also in order to my research assistant Gary Mounce for checking out biographical information on those persons involved in state and national politics in the setting of the community studied. Finally, I would like to acknowledge the assistance received from members of the Latin American Development Administration Committee of the Comparative Administration Group who, by their questions regarding an earlier version of this study, helped me to re-evaluate the implications of the results reported.

These acknowledgments would not be complete without some mention of the many people in Saragosa who extended their hospitality to my wife, her sister, our children, and me. It was the warmth of their reception which turned a summer's research into a delightful experience. While these individuals will remain unnamed, a word of special thanks goes to Don Pepe.

LAWRENCE S. GRAHAM

Lima, Peru
May, 1967

CONTENTS

INTRODUCTION

This is a study of politics in a small Mexican city in the central highland plateau, some four and a half hours by car from the nation's capital. It is an analysis at the community level of changes in factional control, the general style of politics, and the interactions between external and internal political groups and leaders. Much has been written about Mexican government and politics at the national level; yet very little is known about the dynamics of local politics, and even less is known about the webs of relationships binding together communities with state and national political systems.[1]

The municipality selected for study reported a population of nearly 100,000 in the 1960 census; by 1966 it was claiming 125,000. Of this number 60 per cent resided in the urban area proper, while the remainder lived in surrounding rural areas, either in the countryside or in small population centers. This distinction between the urban center of a municipality and its rural districts should be kept in mind any time one embarks on a study of local government in Latin America. Viewed from a comparative perspective, most local government patterns throughout Latin America combine elements both of the North American urban political community and the county, particularly as it has developed in the southern United States as a governmental unit.

For the purposes of this monograph the name Saragosa will be used to identify the community. While the utility of this study to other social scientists is reduced somewhat by disguising the name of the city, anonymity will be preserved because this was one of the preconditions set during the interview phase of the project in order to establish rapport more quickly with the interviewees. A name of Spanish origin was selected rather than one of Indian character because the municipality is situated in an area of Mexico where the culture is predominantly Spanish American in character, rather than Indo-American. Certainly the mestizo is present, but the dominant cultural patterns are more Hispanic in derivation

1. Eric R. Wolf, "Aspects of Group Relations in a Complex Society: Mexico," in Richard N. Adams and Dwight B. Heath (eds.), *Contemporary Cultures and Societies of Latin America* (New York: Random House, 1965), p. 86.

than a blend of Indian and European elements. And the value system of this community is shaped by a conservative Roman Catholicism reminiscent of the sort found in the small cities and towns of central Spain.

Three or four decades ago, the life of the community was torn apart by the struggle between revolutionary forces asserting a new order and Church-oriented groups rallying behind the symbol of Christ the King. Today it is an integrated community in the sense that the stark divisions created by the Revolution have largely disappeared. In their place has emerged a blend of the revolutionary ideology institutionalized by the Partido Revolucionario Institucional (PRI) and a highly conservative community leadership drawn from among local businessmen and professionals.

Saragosa is situated in the heart of one of highland Mexico's lush agricultural valleys. Its economy has always been tied closely to agriculture and its style of life has remained provincial. Before the Revolution it prospered as a small residential and commercial center for the local landowning aristocracy. During the Revolution and afterward with the land reform program, it suffered—as did so many other parts of Mexico. Then, gradually, agricultural production resumed its earlier importance under a new land system where roughly 60 per cent of the surrounding land was held by small rural communities (ejidos) and the remaining 40 per cent by small landowners, and Saragosa prospered once again.

While the growth of two nearby communities has been more spectacular in recent years as a consequence of new highways and incipient industrialization, Saragosa, too, has experienced growth and change, although of a different kind. Because its development as an urban center has been based on its function as a trading, banking, educational, and residential center for the surrounding rural area, its expansion has been more gradual. As a whole it is a highly presentable and well-developed community. Certainly urban services are not all that one would wish, but they are quite adequate for the core areas of the city. In contrast, the larger of the two nearby communities, where change has become such a characteristic, reflects a certain disorder. Construction is going on everywhere; the streets are in constant disarray due to the installation of a new water system; and there is the contrast of the traditional and the modern as new residences and buildings make their appearance. It is only in the last few years that Saragosa has seen

2

its competitor move ahead in size, income, employment, and prosperity. This, coupled with the rapid growth of a second nearby community, primarily because of the construction of a refinery, has awakened many residents of Saragosa to the need to revitalize the city.

1. RESEARCH DESIGN

This study of Saragosa was undertaken with four explicit objectives in mind: to study the decision-making structure of a Mexican community; to determine the scope of government in relation to the economic and social systems of the community; to provide an analysis of variations in political style at the local level over a fixed time span and in so doing to test the degree of pluralism or elitism in the community (that is, the degree to which power is concentrated or dispersed among its members); and to obtain data on community politics in a Mexican city that could be used for comparative purposes in testing propositions developed in the analysis of community politics in the United States.[1] These objectives were limited by one basic requirement: the research had to be completed within three months.

To insure clarity of purpose, several assumptions were made. First, it was assumed that power was to be conceptualized in this context essentially as a system of social relationships. This implied the existence of a "certain ongoing network of fairly stable subsystems, activated by social, economic, ethnic, religious, and friendship ties and claims."[2] As such, power was conceived of as a consequence of relations among individuals within a particular institutional context and not as an element in and of itself that was identifiable. This assumption, in turn, led to the second, for if power was to be observed within a particular institutional context, it would require the use of systems theory in the analysis of politics at the community level. Hence, it was assumed that the community studied could be considered a subsystem within the broader framework of state and national politics. This notion of the community as an identifiable system meant further that the traditional divisions between what is public and private, and what is politics and administration, would be insufficient. It was thus assumed that there would be no clear-cut boundaries between that which is private and public; instead, issues would fall along a continuum ranging from public to

1. Robert E. Agger, Daniel Goldrich, and Bert E. Swanson, *The Rulers and the Ruled: Political Power and Impotence in American Communities*, pp. 2-3, 37-40; Robert Presthus, *Men at the Top: A Study in Community Power*, pp. 42-45.
2. Presthus, p. 5.

private. Similarly, it was assumed that there would be no dichotomy between politics and administration. This would mean that while there would be political and administrative institutions, their functions would be more clearly defined if they were conceived of as falling at various points along a continuum ranging from the political, where there would be a maximum of conflict over the determination of a particular policy or action, to the administrative, where the carrying out of a policy or action would be purely routine in character.[3]

Within this framework four variables were isolated: the inclusiveness or exclusiveness of the decision-making structure, the economic structure of the community, the extent of extra-community control over economic groups, and the extent of extra-community political control over the resolution of local issues. Linked together these variables were stated in the form of a central proposition, based on an earlier study by Ruth McQuown. The purpose here was to take her hypothesis, developed for the analysis of community politics in a southern city of the United States, and test it in another cultural setting.

As restated the central hypothesis reads: "The extent to which the political decision-making structure of a community includes all of the major economic groups in the community will be determined by the character of the economic structure, the extra- or intra-community locations of control over the economic groups . . . the political skills of these groups," and the extent of extra-community political control over the resolution of local issues.[4] While the last variable, the extent of extra-community political control, was not included in the McQuown study, it was deemed essential in this case because of the centralized nature of the Mexican political system.

This hypothesis seeks to establish a relationship between three independent variables (the economic structure of the community, the extent of extra-community control over economic groups, and the extent of extra-community political control over the resolution of local issues) and a dependent variable: the exclusiveness or inclusiveness of the decision-making structure. Involved here is an intervening variable—the political skills of the economic groups and

3. Fred W. Riggs, remarks at the Comparative Administration Group Conference, College Park, Md., April, 1966.
4. Ruth McQuown, William R. Hamilton, and Michael P. Schneider, *The Political Restructuring of a Community*, p. 3.

leaders in the community—which likewise is based on the Mc-Quown study. The articulation of demands by various economic groups and their leaders in the community and their participation in the local decision-making process is conditioned or limited by their ability to use political symbols and techniques. Because these skills are concerned with the conversion of sources of political power into political action, they are conceived of as intervening factors.

While this project was not intended to be a rigorous power structure study, two related propositions pertaining to community power structures[5] were also tested. These come from Robert Presthus' study of two New York towns. The first of these propositions concerns the relationship between leadership elements and the community's economic resources.

> In communities with limited leadership and economic resources the power structure will be more likely to be dominated by political leaders, whereas in those with more fulsome internal resources it will probably be dominated by economic leaders. However . . . over an extended period of time economic leaders will probably dispose the most powerful role in community affairs. This is because their characteristic bases of power are relatively more stable than those of political leaders who most often depend upon *office* as the major bases of their power. In addition economic leaders in both communities typically enjoy higher SES [socioeconomic] rankings which means that they possess more of the resources typically required for the exercise of power, including more education and income, higher class and prestige status. . . . These attributes, combined with their access to financial and economic resources of local banks and corporations, provide them greater continuity of leadership.[6]

The second proposition states a relationship between community leadership patterns and the degree of citizen participation in local

---

5. Throughout this paper the term "community power structure" will be used to mean "a representation of selected aspects of political power relations over a specified time period. Alternatively, a community power structure is a representation of selected patterns of the organization that produces the political decisions which determine the scope of government for a specific time period"—Robert E. Agger, Daniel Goldrich, and Bert E. Swanson, *The Rulers and the Ruled: Political Power and Impotence in American Communities*, p. 51.

6. Presthus, pp. 410-11.

issues. "There is a positive relation between the degree to which a community is socially integrated and the manner in which it solves its problems, i.e. through some citizen participation in crucial local decisions, or through more centralized control and action by a few hyperactive leaders."[7]

7. *Ibid.*, p. 412.

2. METHODOLOGY

The techniques used in the field were two: newspaper research and in-depth interviewing.

The local press was consulted for a period extending from January, 1964, through June, 1966. The original research design called for using the newspaper for a full five years, but unanticipated problems in using this source were such that the time span was reduced to two and a half years. The newspaper was frustrating to work with because of its incompleteness. In a small provincial Mexican town there is little enough to report simply because the pace of life is much slower and there is a feeling of isolation from the events of the outside world. The issues which properly can be called local are few in number. Yet not even these are always reportable—either because the solution of the problem is dependent on sources external to the community or because the issues are considered too controversial to handle.

Regardless of these difficulties, the newspaper did provide useful information of several types. First, it provided familiarity with the community in terms of its political, social, and economic life. Thus, it was possible to develop a preliminary list of visible local influentials, identified on the basis of political, social, and economic positions held. Likewise it provided a checklist for local organizations and associations. Second, the press suggested preliminary patterns of relationships tying the life of the city in with that of state and nation. Third, the newspaper reflected the provincial character of the community and the prevailing social ethic. For example, on one occasion the newspaper admonished the citizenry to turn out in great numbers to honor properly a forthcoming procession of the community's patron saint through the city's streets. Finally, while the press did not supply an issue-orientation toward political events, it did suggest enough about the political life of the community to serve as a reference point in determining issues which might be studied. Having first become familiar with the local press, newspaper research made it possible during the interviewing phase of the project to develop a list of issues offering insight into the decision-making structure of the community.

Once newspaper research was completed, five exploratory interviews were held. The original purpose here was to select five recent issues from a list prepared on the basis of newspaper research and to test the questionnaire. Once again, the research design had to be modified. Because the local press was incomplete as a source for identifying salient issues, a list of potential issues was introduced into the interview schedule during the first five interviews and was repeated at random during the first half of the interviewing phase of the project. This check list was dropped finally because it neither contributed to acquiring new data nor did it assist the researcher in keeping a focus for the interviews. As a matter of fact, more often than not it provided a mechanism through which those interviewed could more easily avoid direct probes.[1]

An interview panel was compiled from three sources: clues obtained in newspaper research, visible political leaders, and attributed influentials identified as the interviews progressed. The initial list was based entirely on newspaper sources. As the interviewing progressed, the list was scaled down considerably and a few new names were added on the basis of participation in the five issues examined or socioeconomic standing in the community. By and large there was considerable overlapping so that these three sources of information did not supply conflicting names; instead, the same names kept turning up with a high degree of frequency. For example, with two exceptions all the mayors since 1942 would have been identified as attributed influentials, on the basis of their activities as local businessmen or professionals.

Forty-three interviews were completed (although two of these did not focus on the interview-guide); two individuals refused to discuss any matters pertaining to local politics; and ten individuals were not contacted successfully—either because they were traveling abroad during the time the study was conducted or because of the difficulty of getting them to set a time for the interview. Of the forty-three interviews completed, the time involved averaged approximately sixty minutes. However, there was considerable variation in the length of individual interviews. One or two lasted no more than twenty minutes, while others were broken into a series of visits totaling some two and a half or three hours.

In-depth interviewing in the personalistic world of the Mexican community was not without its difficulties. For the most part the citizens of Saragosa were not accustomed to having outsiders con-

1. See Appendix III for a list of potential issues.

9

duct interviews regarding local politics. Quite early in the project it became apparent that those who participated in the local decision-making process were much more limited in number than might be assumed for a city of this size. The whole atmosphere was very much that of a small town and those who had a knowledge of local issues, more often than not, were reluctant to discuss them in much detail with an outsider, particularly a North American. More than once the fear was expressed that the project would become another *Children of Sánchez* (Oscar Lewis) and would unfavorably reflect the political life of the city as they felt the *Children of Sánchez* did on the social behavior of the Mexican people. The initial contact in many cases became something of an attempt to sell a bill of goods, to convince the individuals that the interviewer represented no threat. Regardless of these attempts, the incumbent mayor never did accept the project as legitimate. More than once his polite but firm refusal to discuss local politics in depth—and a communication of this attitude to others—presented an obstacle in completing the interview panel.

Because of this problem and the relatively small number of people with a reputation for influence or with the sort of experience that would classify them as active influentials, emphasis was placed on establishing rapport or *confianza* with a limited number of persons, rather than on obtaining a higher number of interviews that would be statistically relevant. The success of the interviews conducted bore a direct relationship to the amount of rapport established with the interviewee. But the more rapport was established, the more difficult it became to conduct a structured interview. Some of the most valuable interviews took the form of conversations over a cup of coffee or a beer. As the study proceeded it became clear that confidence was much easier to establish once the interviewer left off note-taking and began to reconstruct the interview after he had finished with the interviewee.

A further complicating factor was the gap between formal political institutions and the legal structure established by the PRI, on the one hand, and the realities of Mexican politics, on the other. To the degree that rapport and confidence were established, the interview passed from the theoretical and the legalistic to a discussion of the individual's own perception of politics as he saw it from his vantage point and his participation, if any, in this process.

While the time span covered by the interviews extended over

twenty-five years, the issues selected for detailed analysis focused on events occurring primarily within a two-and-a-half-year period. Since these issues reflected only a small cross-sampling of local politics and provided a single perspective, a major part of the questionnaire was directed to topics suggesting the underlying power structure of the community. Contrary to what was expected, the relationships uncovered were not so much internal to the community as they were external, pointing to ties integrating the political life of Saragosa with that of the rest of the country. The fact that the interview data focus on the brokerage function of local political leaders and how they maintain tension between community-oriented and nation-oriented groups within a single subsystem[2] was an unanticipated consequence that was not properly appreciated until the results were written up.

The lack of easily identifiable issues in Saragosa and the low degree of issue-orientation toward politics among the respondents was the major methodological problem faced in carrying out the project. This in turn raises the question of whether some of the techniques developed for the analysis of community politics in the United States are transferrable to areas outside the boundaries of our culture. The relevant question to ask here is to what extent such criteria as formal position, attribution of power, and the issue-orientation can provide accurate information in the Latin American setting.[3] The findings reported in the following pages suggest that these are relevant criteria if the researcher is flexible in developing his own ways of getting at this information and adapts these criteria to the field situation.

The gaps in the newspaper account of politics in Saragosa indicate the absence of one of the data sources available in the United States through which to apply these techniques. Yet, as has already been shown, this situation which is repeated often in the Latin American press does not mean that newspaper research should be neglected as a source of information in the study of community politics.

Similarly, the lack of easily identified issues and a low degree of issue-orientation toward politics should not lead to the conclusion that this is primarily a consequence of a cultural setting different

2. Wolf, pp. 97-98.
3. Robert T. Daland, A Strategy for Research in Comparative Urban Administration, pp. 22-23.

11

from that of the United States. As so often happens, we are dealing with a mixture of factors. On the one hand, politics in Saragosa has much in common with small-town politics in the United States. As Banfield and Wilson have pointed out, there really is little at stake in the politics of a small town. In such a setting the function of politics is "less to resolve issues than, by suppressing them, to enable people to get along with each other while living together in very close contact. The leaders of the town depend for support upon personal associations and friendships and being 'good fellows,' not upon interest groups and organized constituencies. . . . Where everyone is in frequent face-to-face contact with almost everyone else, it is essential that all be on good terms."[4] However, when conflict develops and the arrangements designed to suppress conflict break down, "politics in the small community tends to be more bitter, more divisive, and more explosive than politics in the large city."[5] On the other hand, if we examine population figures, Saragosa is not a small town by North American standards. The explanation here lies in the transitional character of politics in the Mexican setting. Joined together in the same community were individuals who as members of a traditional rural society were generally non-participant and others who as members of a town subculture were urban-oriented, literate, and participant in the social, political, and economic life of the community.[6]

4. Edward C. Banfield and James Q. Wilson, *City Politics*, p. 25
5. *Ibid.*, p. 26.
6. For a discussion of the traditional-transitional-modern syndrome see Daniel Lerner, *The Passing of Traditional Society: Modernizing the Middle East*, especially p. 50.

3. THE INSTITUTIONAL
FRAMEWORK

Saragosa is the third most important *municipio* in the state where it is located, if the criteria of population and revenues provided for state and national government are used. It is the seat of a federal electoral district consisting of four adjacent *municipios*. Within the setting of state politics, it is likewise the seat of an electoral district, although in this case only three of the four *municipios* just mentioned are included. It is also one of the sixteen judicial seats (*partidos judiciales*) into which the state is divided.

The municipal law (the *ley orgánica municipal*) is a piece of state legislation, issued in the form of a decree, dating from 1918, that establishes the same legal framework for all the *municipios* in the state. In theory this law provides for a mayor-council form of government, one in which specific responsibilities and duties are given to the local town councils, the *ayuntamientos*. In comparison with local governmental patterns in the United States one might describe the way this system has functioned as a strong-mayor, weak-council form of government. In theory a great deal is made of the free municipality. Reality, however, is quite different and, as will become obvious in the succeeding pages, the way in which local governmental responsibilities are carried out depends to a considerable extent on who the governor is at a given moment and on his relations with the federal government.

While it is the municipal law which defines the legal framework of the *municipio* and spells out the division of responsibilities between the mayor and the council, it is the state constitution, in its revised form, that regulates public office in the *municipios*. The constitution quite explicitly establishes a strong council form of government: "The *ayuntamientos* will administer collectively the affairs of the *municipios* and the president of the corporation will direct its deliberations and will serve as the executor of its accords." It subsequently limits the period of office for the municipal president, the councilmen (the *regidores*), and the *síndico* (an elected official who handles legal affairs for the *municipio*) to a period of three years, with the limitation that no one individual can be reelected in the succeeding period. This is an institutional factor of

13

some importance because, regardless of its democratic intent, it has helped to maintain a fragmented power structure in a community where the local leadership showed signs of coalescing (until recently).

A third legal document further defining the institutional setting for Saragosa is the state's electoral code. Besides setting the dates and the procedure for local elections, it controls the number of *regidores* each *municipio* may have. Article 102 of this code stipulates that the group of *municipios* to which Saragosa belongs will be governed by a municipal president, a *síndico*, and nine *regidores*.

Finally, since the party system in existence in Mexico may be classified as a dominant one-party system, the 1965 party statutes of the PRI further define the institutional setting for local government in Saragosa. Without going into detail, these statutes in Chapter XVIII provide an elaborate system for internal democracy along sector lines existing in the national party: the campesino or agrarian sector, the worker sector, and the popular sector into which are grouped a variety of small business and professional groups. While in theory these three sectors are equals, in practice the sector dominating local politics in Saragosa is the popular sector. In contrast, in regional politics it is the agrarian sector which has become more important.

The significance of the institutional framework provided by the local PRI organization cannot be overemphasized, for it supplies the crucial tension-maintaining mechanism for handling external and internal pressures on the community. As will become apparent in the following section, the basic pattern of issue-resolution is upward and outward, and it is not conditioned by the building of agreement within the community among various cliques and groups. What the local PRI organization offers is a dual communications and mobility network. One is apparent in the preeminence of the popular sector in the town and it extends upward through the state capital to the national government; the other is built upon the importance of the agrarian sector in the federal electoral district of which Saragosa is a part. This latter network has received new impetus only recently. This is because in the last election for federal deputy the Partido de Acción Nacional (PAN) emerged as a serious contender. A majority in the city voted for the PAN candidate, while the surrounding rural areas of the *municipio*, joined by four other rural

14

municipios in the electoral district, supplied the vote which allowed the PRI candidate to win officially by a small majority. At the same time the bitterness of the local PAN organization against the outcome of the election was lessened by having the PAN candidate appointed as a federal deputy under the new law guaranteeing minority parties some representation in congress.[1]

These institutional arrangements, joined with the realities of political power, insure for the foreseeable future the preeminence of the PRI in the Saragosa district.

1. This law is stated in the form of an amendment to the Constitution. It stipulates that a party receiving at least 2.5 per cent of the national vote in 1964 would receive a minimum of five deputies, with additional seats for each 0.5 per cent more votes up to twenty deputies. See Robert E. Scott, "Mexico: The Established Revolution," in Lucian W. Pye and Sidney Verba (eds.), *Political Culture and Political Development* (Princeton, N.J.: Princeton University Press, 1965), p. 370.

4. THE ISSUES

The five issues singled out as meaningful in analyzing Saragosa's decision-making process were, first, the need to acquire new sources of income for the city and the attraction of new industries and companies to the immediate area; second, the attempt by the rector and the council of the state university to abolish a branch of the university located in Saragosa; third, the financing of a boulevard built through the middle of the city; fourth, the construction of a dam benefiting Saragosa and the surrounding region; and, fifth, fluctuation in agricultural prices and the attempt to develop a cooperative approach to the market among those most concerned.

While everyone interviewed agreed that the creation of new sources of income was essential to resolving the problem created by an influx of individuals from the surrounding countryside in search of employment and the benefits of urban life, most of them pointed out that very little had been accomplished, regardless of a great deal of discussion and attention given to the matter. The major reason cited was that decisions determining the coming of a new business to the area came from sources outside the community. It was noted repeatedly that there was little local initiative in these matters. What initiative there was had been sporadic and poorly coordinated. The notion of local businessmen banding together into an organization for this purpose or utilizing the existing framework provided by the Chamber of Commerce (CANACO) or the Chamber for Industries (CANACINTRA) was completely unknown in the experience of this city.

There are several explanations for this situation. First, it was indicated that the ties maintained by municipal authorities with the governor of the state and his agencies, and through him with the national government, were crucial. Without the governor's support little could be accomplished. The principal reason cited for dependency on the state government in these matters was that the governor alone had the right to grant tax exemptions to attract new industries or to reduce the tax burden. This sense of helplessness in attracting new enterprises to the region was reinforced by the feeling that Saragosa had lost out in the competition with nearby communities for new enterprises and industries. The fact that an ade-

16

quate industrial base already existed or was being developed in three nearby cities within the state and a fourth in the capital of a state only thirty minutes away by car meant that it would now be even more difficult to attract new plants to the area. To break this cycle it was essential that the city receive aid from the state in the form of subsidization.

Nevertheless, many interviewees made it quite clear that there had been opportunities in the recent past which had not been adequately taken advantage of. Some emphasized the point that Saragosa was simply not interested in just any type of industry. The primary consideration, they maintained, was that new enterprises coming into the area must fit into the community's existing framework and not radically change the nature of the city. These individuals, as well as many others, stressed the fact that the area was preeminently agricultural and that Saragosa's growth over the past three decades was a consequence of its development as a commercial, residential, banking, and educational center for the surrounding region. Joining this was the belief that the city had developed a certain social standing in the southeastern part of the state which they did not wish to see endangered by the arrival of unattractive industries that would destroy the city's present character: what was described as a substantial cultural and social life, provincial perhaps in orientation, yet superior to the surrounding area.

One individual, the member of a clique of young businessmen and professionals dissatisfied with present community leadership, went so far as to explain the failure to attract new sources of income for the city as essentially the responsibility of those who wielded power in the community: the agricultural-business interests who had for so long dominated the city and who had worked out a very comfortable arrangement for the sharing of power through the local PRI structure. He maintained that frequent discussion of the need for new enterprises and failure to take action should not be viewed entirely as a consequence of the fact that effective decisions were made outside the community. This was because the community traditionally had been considered a major element in state politics and had been successful in maintaining access to the governor of the state. Of course, he said, this access had fluctuated over the past twenty years, but there were periods during which local authorities could have established the necessary contacts had they so desired. He insisted that the major explanation lay in the preeminence of a local elite and its desire not to have the city develop a new, competing economic basis which would raise wages, force payment of the minimum wage established for the region, and possibly challenge their control of the community.

The interest of local businessmen in not having the wage structure of the community changed was repeatedly cited by others as one of the factors conditioning local interest in the arrival of new businesses or industries. Many, for example, referred to the failure of a new refinery to locate in the municipality, in spite of its original interest in Saragosa, in these terms. The major concern of many local businessmen was that the refinery as a government enterprise would pay considerably higher wages and that it would endanger their own operations and force them to compete unfavorably in the prevailing labor market. Others, either concurrently or separately, referred to the fear that such an operation would introduce into the community undesirable working-class elements and upset what they considered to be very amicable labor-management relations. These individuals likewise stressed the importance of Saragosa's maintaining its small town, provincial, aristocratic character.

Land costs were another factor in explaining the failure of several companies to locate in the community. Besides the petroleum refinery, Carnation and Campbell's were at one time interested in Saragosa. All three found the cost of available land in the municipality too high in contrast with the land available in other communities either at no cost or at a minimal price. This situation stems from the fact that the area is nearly all agricultural with the land immediately surrounding the city presently under cultivation, either on the basis of communal holdings or through small privately owned farms. More often than not it has been impossible, even when local authorities have wanted to attract a company, to get the owners of the land to name a price acceptable to the firm.

Yet, regardless of this situation, several new companies have located successfully in the community in recent years—Petrochemicals, Inc., a subsidiary of a United States corporation and a joint venture supported by Mexican and North American capital; a seed-processing factory; and Fertilizers, Inc., a plant and central office operated in Mexico by a major United States concern. Why did they come to Saragosa? In every case the major reason given was their own interest initially in the community. This interest stemmed from the excellent communications available from Saragosa by highway and railroad with other areas of the country, the desirable nature of the community as a place of residence for their management, and the availability of water and electric power.

In the case of Petrochemicals, Inc., additional factors were the proximity of Saragosa to a new petroleum refinery, its location on a major gas line, and the encouragement given the organization by national and state governments. A company official stated that the construction of the new plant in Saragosa, which took place in 1964 and represented an initial investment of 40 million pesos—or $3.2 million—could not be viewed entirely as a consequence of immediate circumstances. The decision to locate in Saragosa had come about as a consequence of the policy of the national government to stimulate major industrial concerns in the Federal District to decentralize their operations.

The factors influencing Fertilizers, Inc., to locate in Saragosa were similar. The nearby presence of a refinery was important, since in plant operations the firm depended on some of the by-products produced by the refinery. Other elements were the availability of labor and the relative absence of unionization, the existence of excellent communications, and the decision to relocate the company's main offices in Mexico by moving them from one of the border cities to Saragosa.

Campbell's also should be included here, even though it is not located within the confines of the city or its immediate environs. The company was interested in locating in Saragosa because of the agricultural nature of the region, but was unable to find land reasonably priced. So it settled for a tract a few minutes away in a neighboring municipality which is entirely rural in character. While most of the employees in the plant come from the surrounding countryside, the company's officials all live in Saragosa.

Within Saragosa there were a limited number of individuals who were directly concerned with acquiring new sources of income for the city or who were involved in the decisions of the firms cited to come to Saragosa. In each case the principal figure was the mayor. For instance, once Fertilizers, Inc., and Petrochemicals, Inc., developed an interest in locating in Saragosa, company officials entered into contact with municipal authorities. The major service provided by the local political leadership was the arranging of a suitable price for the tracts of land needed by the companies. The mayor served as a broker between the private interests owning the land and company officials who desired to purchase it at a reasonable price. Yet even the participation of local political leaders was limited, for while virtually all municipal presidents since World War II devoted attention to this issue, the only real success achieved came about during the two most recent administrations (1961-63, 1964-66) and this was a consequence of factors external to the community. Beyond the mayors in these two administrations (mayors A and B)[1] only three individuals were cited with any regularity. At the time of the interviewing they were members of the town council and the Comité Pro-Industrialización, an organization created by the incumbent municipal president (mayor A) to stimulate local economic development. One was the manager of a beer-distributing concern, the second a manager of the Pepsi-Cola plant, the third the owner of a canning factory created by the person's own initiative. A fourth person named independently of these three men was the director (the *secretario*) of the local CANACINTRA. All four were primarily concerned with the acquisition of basic data of the sort that a company locating in the city would need to know, but as of the end of August, 1966, neither the committee nor the local CANACINTRA had produced a body of useful material.

The failure of members of the local business community to participate in the resolution of this issue of how to expand the economic base of the community, or to establish an effective cooperative framework, led the author to re-examine the interview data for a further explanation. The data accrued suggest that the nature of personal relations is of great importance. These relationships are best summarized in the language of one respondent, a prominent local businessman and a former municipal president (mayor C). The way new firms come into a city such as Saragosa, he said, is through personal contacts. So-and-so has a friend in the community with whom he enters into contact and through him obtains information from his close circle of friends. The basic decisions are thus made within a group of persons where each can be assured of *confianza*. In this respect each decision to bring in a new company or enterprise or to work with feelers that are sent out by an organization external to the community may well involve a different circle of intimate friends—hence the lack of coordination of such efforts.

Another dimension is the importance of *confianza* among mem-

1. For a listing of the mayors in office from 1942 through 1966, see the chart in Chapter 6.

bers of the town council. By and large, municipal presidents during the period studied were able to have their council members chosen from among close associates. Each municipal president brought with him into office a different group of close friends. These men for the most part came from the same general socioeconomic strata. They were businessmen and professionals and were respected members of the community. Yet this did not mean that the predominance of business and professional interests led to a cohesive decision-making structure for dealing with business issues, for within this larger group were a number of personal groups or cliques. This distribution of power within the community is reflected in the fact that every mayor between 1942 and 1967 was either a local businessman or a professionally trained person, surrounded by a different constellation of individuals.[2] Within this period six businessmen, one engineer who was also a local businessman, one medical doctor, and two lawyers served as municipal presidents.

The second issue examined arose first in June, 1965, when it became apparent that the university council did not wish to see further decentralization develop within the state university and sought to abolish Saragosa's Department of Accounting and Business Administration (the Facultad de Contabilidad y Administración de Empresas). Although the program was designed to offer the equivalent of an undergraduate degree at the end of four years, it was at that time only in its second year of operation. The students and the professors participating in the program immediately organized a protest and sought the assistance of municipal authorities. By so doing they hoped to bring pressure to bear on the state government and the university to see that their interests were protected.

The school's students and professors were able to receive full support from the municipal president (mayor A). They appealed to him on several counts. He was one of the founders of the Preparatory and Professional School, the institute in which the business administration program had been developed; he had served as the director of the school in the past; he had always maintained a great deal of interest in the growth and the development of the school; and he had access to the state governor. The mayor promised that he and his administration would do all in their power to see that the

2. For recurring patterns of participation in local government in Saragosa, see Appendix IV.

current program would be continued and allowed to develop fully. The local paper on July 8 reported assurances from the governor that the program would not be abolished. Exactly one month later the university council made public its decision to close the school of business administration and to remove the director. This brought an immediate counter-statement from the governor. The director would not be removed and the program would continue. On the twenty-fourth of the month, the university council repeated its original stand. So far as they were concerned, the director was fired, the program was nullified, and if the students who had spent two years in the program wished to receive credit for their work, they would have to apply immediately for admission to the program in public accounting which would be allowed to continue in Saragosa. Two days later, an announcement appeared in the paper stating that a new director had been named for the school and that the governor had approved his nomination and had asserted that the program was still very much alive. There was no further reference to the affair until February 2 of the next year when a notice appeared to the effect that the university council had authorized the creation of a school of business administration (the Escuela de Licenciado en Administración de Empresas). There was no doubt after this date that the program would be allowed to continue and expand. The issue had come to an end.

While the course of events is fairly clear from the newspaper account, no attempt was made to clarify why this issue had come about. For this information it was necessary to rely exclusively on the interview data. According to the former director and other citizens in the community with an immediate interest in the affair, the problem had arisen because the university council had never recognized the program officially. But the director had received authorization from the governor to initiate the program and the rector had provided funds to pay the salaries of new professors brought in to teach courses in business administration and to meet other operational costs. Then, without warning, under the pretext of illegality, the university council had attempted to abolish the program.

What were some of the reasons for this action and who were the major participants? The interviewees maintained repeatedly that the state university had become concerned over the possibility of setting a precedent for the decentralization of its functions. Many viewed the action in terms of vested interests in the state capital.

This was a capital which already had seen other population centers in the state bypass it in terms of commercial and industrial activity. Since that city could rely only on its function as the state's administrative and political center, as the site of the state university, and as a place for tourism, it did not wish to weaken its economic base further. Others referred to a personal conflict that had developed between the school's director and the rector and perceived the action in personalistic terms. The rector simply wanted to see the director removed.

On the surface, the response of the community was such that it appeared that many different individuals and groups were involved. The newspaper account stressed the spontaneous reactions of those affected: the professors of the school, the student body, and business and professional interests in the city. A protest meeting was held, a delegation to the governor named, and a number of new associations emerged devoted to the purpose of bringing pressure to bear on the state and university officials concerned.

Yet the interview material does not demonstrate that any of this activity had any real effect. There were simply no direct channels of access open to them. What it does indicate is the small number of people involved in the decision-making process, and their response to the interests articulated determined whether the matter would receive proper representation before state officials. The key figure once again was the municipal president. Without his action and his access to the governor, every one of the interviewees asserted, it would have been impossible to protect the school's existence. The other direct participants were close associates of the mayor, men upon whom he knew he could rely. One of these was a school companion of his who was a member of the university council. He was to become the school's new director. The other two citizens were businessmen. One contributed funds to the endeavor and the other, a man who held a degree in business administration and was actively involved in the school, offered his time and his services.

In the final analysis, the decision to continue the program came from outside the community. It was made by the governor and the university council in the state capital. Even the action of the mayor —the community's major participant—was limited by this condition. His basic function was to represent the community's interests. And in this capacity he was joined by Saragosa's representative to the state assembly, a man who was assembly president during the summer of 1966. The only channel through which interests could be articulated was a political one, maintained and operated by the state PRI organization.

While the search for new sources of income for the municipality and the school program in business administration were identifiable as issues on the basis of newspaper research, the third issue received no attention whatsoever from the local press. Yet this issue, which dealt with the payment of construction costs for a boulevard built through the middle of the city, was probably the single most explosive affair to emerge in Saragosa in recent years. Not only was there no mention of the affair in the paper, it was also difficult to establish through interviewing exactly what had given rise to the problem and who were the organizations and individuals most active. What led the interviewer into this issue unsuspectingly was the obvious existence of the boulevard, the excellent quality of street paving and lighting in the central areas of the city, and the discussion of the problem of urban services in the initial interviews.

The time period concerned extends from December, 1962, when the construction of the boulevard was begun, to its completion in December, 1964. However, the issue of its financing did not emerge until the end of this period. At the outset, it appears, all were quite pleased to see the governor initiate, under a general project devoted to urbanization of the state, the construction of the boulevard and undertake paving, guttering, sewerage, and lighting projects in the center of the city.

Expectations were very high that the governor's plan would contribute greatly to meeting Saragosa's needs. Little had been done to improve urban services since the state government had imposed changes along these lines in the mid-1930's. So the story goes, the town council at that time took a firm stand against the changes proposed by the governor and to express its opposition declared itself in permanent session. While the councilmen were meeting, the machinery sent by the governor arrived and the urban improvement project was begun despite council protests.

The plan submitted by the state government in 1962 called for construction of a major artery cutting through the city, one block south of the central plaza and major commercial area. This artery was to be in the form of a four-lane highway which would not only make it easier to reach the center of Saragosa, but also would tie in directly with a major highway extending west from Mexico City that passed through the community. The plans also called for the opening of another major thoroughfare, on a north-south axis, which would tie in with highways extending north and south from Saragosa and provide a more effective link with the principal east-west route for the area. This latter phase of the project was never begun, nor were other works of urbanization in the planning stages ever inaugurated. The escalation of the issue over payment for the boulevard reached such a point that public protests broke out, relations with the governor of the state were strained, and the municipal president (mayor A) was discredited in the eyes of the citizens of his city. Many of the sensitivities raised by the conflict still were very much alive in the summer of 1966 when the interviewing was conducted. More than any other factor, this incident can be used to explain the defensiveness of many of those interviewed when the topic of local politics was raised.

The cost of the boulevard, according to the mayor's report for the year ending 1965, was 27,223,577.43 pesos (or roughly $2,217,886). According to a decree issued by the governor the entire cost of the project was to be borne by the city. As many of those interviewed were to point out, this in itself violated a federal law stipulating that when public works are undertaken by a state government, 40 per cent of the cost is to be borne by the state government, the remainder by the municipality. This situation was aggravated by the fact that the time period in which the city had to pay its obligations to the state government was reduced from ten years to two. Furthermore, the brunt of the burden was not distributed equally. Those who owned property affected by the construction of the boulevard were to pay the largest assessments, an assessment based on the increased value of the property as a result of the construction of the road. Even though the property was purchased at a liberal price in comparison to the value of the land prior to construction, the sums levied in the form of a tax called the "plus-valia" were confiscatory for the majority of the citizens immediately concerned. These people were not, for the most part, among the more prosperous inhabitants of the city, for the principal part of the boulevard passed through a very poor area of the city. Displaced from their homes either because their property was taken over entirely by the state or because what remained was subject to such a high tax that they could no longer hold it, these families had no place to go. Frustrated because of their inability to communicate their demands

25

through political channels, public demonstration became their only alternative.

The first stage of the protests was confined to those most immediately affected. These people banded together in an association to protect their interests and called on two substantial members of the community to assist them. One of these men was a prosperous businessman who spent most of his time in Mexico City where he had other business interests to look after. He was affected because the western exit of the boulevard passed through a subdivision he was developing into a residential area for more prosperous members of the community. It was not an area where the local elite resided—that was located around a park in the northeastern section of the city—but the construction was such that it was far beyond the means of the average citizen in Saragosa. The second individual was a former medical doctor who had abandoned his practice to devote attention to the development of insecticides for the area. He had a reputation as a local influential, dating back some thirty years.

The organization raised sufficient funds to undertake a study of the governor's project. Besides establishing the facts mentioned, its members discovered that not only was the cost of the boulevard far in excess of costs for similar road construction in the Federal District, but also entailed was manipulation of the original bidding on the project. In this connection a second violation of existing laws was determined. The governor had not opened the bids on the boulevard to the public at large, but had only accepted bids from two companies. In both of these companies he owned important shares, if not the controlling interest.

On the basis of this knowledge, members of the organization formed a commission to see the proper municipal and state authorities and to demand a readjustment in the financing of the boulevard. According to one of the major participants, it was impossible for the commission to see the municipal president; he would not make himself available. This individual interpreted the mayor's action as a consequence of his desire to keep the matter as quiet as possible so as not to offend the governor and strain his ties with him. A contrary point of view comes from those on the town council. They maintained that the municipal president in consultation with the council did everything in his power to meet the demands of the group and to keep the matter from coming into the open where it could do little but damage the best interests of Saragosa. Whichever of these two views is correct remains a moot question, but what did happen is that public demonstrations broke out in the city and the municipal president became the immediate object of attack. The demonstrators viewed him as the governor's agent in the community.

Apparently at this stage a third major figure became involved in the affair. This was the federal deputy for PAN in the Saragosa district. Up until this juncture he had avoided participating—in deference to a request by the aforementioned doctor who asked him to stay out so that the protest would not take on political overtones in an election year. With the entrance of the deputy into the affair, the doctor withdrew and the PAN representative became the focal figure for the groups opposing the governor's stance. According to the deputy, he found his participation desirable at this point. As the leader of the opposition party in the district, he felt that he could help to channel the protests in the direction of some solution. Shortly thereafter, the governor called him to the state capital to answer for a speech he had delivered in the national congress attacking the governor and his urbanization plan for the state.

Protests continued in Saragosa. A public meeting was held in the central plaza—violence ensued and the state police were sent in to stop the demonstrations. According to the deputy, he was in the governor's office when the protests reached this final point and at this juncture the governor agreed to receive the commission from Saragosa. Those involved in the protest pointed out that the commission had attempted to see the governor earlier, but until this stage was reached he was unwilling to grant them an interview.

The governor received the commission and stated that he would correct the situation. While the PAN deputy claimed that the governor never kept his agreement with the commission, the payments question was dropped entirely. And, until the end of August, 1966, no attempt had been made to force any of the citizens of Saragosa to pay for the work undertaken by the state. Apparently what the governor did under the circumstances was to pay only for the interest on the loans obtained for the work out of legislative appropriations in the general budget. This total sum was large, given the fact that other urbanization projects were underway on a grand scale throughout the state.

This matter of state finances remained a delicate issue. Both the

PAN and the PRI federal deputies, regardless of the fact that they were political opponents, agreed that the governor's plan had thrown the state's finances into chaos and that he had assumed obligations for the future far beyond the state's capacity to pay. They also indicated that the demonstrations in Saragosa were part of a larger reaction that had taken place throughout the state in protest against the urbanization plan and a general tax increase. As an example of the sad state of finances, the PAN deputy cited the following figures. Present tax revenues for the state were 130 million pesos. The governor had just sent to the state assembly a request for a budget supplement of 398 million pesos for the year. The obligations already facing the state due to the governor's expenditures on the plan amounted to 100 million pesos. And the interest on this debt was running between 6 and 7 per cent per year—or some 6 million pesos.

A PRI official in Mexico City from Saragosa state, with access to decision-makers at the national level, went so far as to define the urbanization plan exclusively as the governor's own operation. He said that it was only two years ago that the party had become interested in the financial side of the program, for until that point the governor was never asked how the program would be paid for. According to him, 629 million pesos were approved in loans for the undertaking. Then, later, the party found out that the governor also owned the companies. The consequence of the whole affair, from the party's standpoint, was a difficult situation. The governor's actions certainly looked unfavorable for the party at a moment when it was trying to put its own house in order in the state to meet rising competition presented by PAN. Yet, the party's hands as well as those of the President were tied because, after all, the governor was a PRI member and there was no easy way that he could be removed without considerable embarrassment. The best they could do was to minimize the affair and to do their utmost to maintain unity within the state party organization.

Very few people in Saragosa were pleased with the resolution given to the issue. Nearly all of those interviewed, in one way or another, stated that they felt that the affair had turned out very poorly for the city and had damaged the city's standing in the state. Many believed that the outbreak of violence in a community with the standing of Saragosa had tarnished its public image and certainly the whole affair had come close to breaking the community's

28

ties with the governor. These individuals insisted that once you break political communications between a *municipio* and the governor of the state, or subject them to a serious strain, everyone suffers as a consequence. The governor's political career had been stopped for the present—at least in terms of moving into a key position in the national government. The mayor had lost face in nearly everyone's eyes, even though he was not to be blamed directly for the turn of events. Certainly, it pointed out how ineffectual he was in fulfilling his brokerage functions as a municipal president now that a major controversy had occurred and it was clear to everyone how dependent he was on the governor. That in itself, many of the interviewees claimed, was sufficient to halt his political aspirations for the time being. Finally, all urbanization work in the city under the auspices of the state had been suspended (those projects under way were completed and nothing new was begun), and it had become very difficult to seek the governor's assistance in the attraction of new companies to bolster the *municipio*'s economy.

On the other hand, there were those who saw the possibility of some favorable developments for Saragosa over the long run. They were of the opinion that the reaction of the community demonstrated that the citizens were no longer willing to accept without protest the edicts of the governor. In the past perhaps they had seen their municipal presidents imposed from the state capital, but this situation was no longer a tenable one. In the future the governor would have to be more sensitive to the desires of the community in order to build political support. Future political leaders in the state would have to realize that politics was a two-way process and that these leaders must be sensitive to the desires of cities such as Saragosa. Others pointed to the growth of PAN as a loyal opposition and the conception of its role in this area of the state as a minority party contributing to the improvement of the quality of government. Yet there hardly was any widespread consensus on this latter point. Most of the interviewees felt that the local PAN had taken advantage of the situation and that the PAN deputy had intervened to advance his own future.

The remaining issues in Saragosa were minor in comparison to the search for new industry, the school affair, and the protests over the financing of the boulevard. However, the decision-making process was similar in that these decisions were made essentially outside the community. Of these secondary issues, the first pertained to the

29

building of a dam benefiting not only Saragosa but the entire region, the second to the fluctuation in agricultural prices and the attempt to develop a cooperative approach to the market among those most concerned.

The interest in a dam for the region dates back to 1877. Yet, regardless of a seemingly endless series of commissions from Saragosa as well as other cities in the region to governors and presidents, it was only in August, 1965, that construction on a dam finally was undertaken with a completion date set for August or September, 1967. The demands for a dam have centered around two problems: the periodic flooding of farmlands in the immediate vicinity of the river during the rainy season and the absence of sufficient water during the drier months of the year for properties away from the river and others on the slopes of hills and low mountains. The problem of irrigation is perhaps more recent in character, since before the land reform era the region was watered by an extensive irrigation system. Once the land was divided and the large estates disappeared, the irrigation system by and large passed out of existence.

The recent history of the demand for a dam dates largely from the end of World War II. The municipal president for the 1944-45 period (mayor I) headed a commission with the purpose of making overtures to the President of the Republic, Ávila Camacho, and according to him a promise was obtained that the dam would be built. Since nothing came of this promise, all the residents of this area could do was to wait until there was another opportunity when there was a change in presidents. This chance came about during the campaign of Miguel Alemán. As part of his campaign program, a series of round tables were held throughout the country. When he appeared in the southeastern part of the state and met with representatives from the surrounding *municipios*, the perennial topic of the dam was introduced. According to this former mayor who had headed the commission to see Ávila Camacho, Alemán anticipated the request by saying that he knew well what was the problem most current in the minds of the residents of that area of the state. He stated, so this individual reported, that he would not issue a new promise since his predecessor had already authorized the dam, but he would promise that as soon as money was available construction on the dam would begin. Still, however, construction was not undertaken.

When the topic was raised once again during the next administration—that of Adolfo Ruiz Cortines—the reply was a familiar one. There simply were not sufficient funds available, given the existence of more important priorities for public works in other areas of the country.

In June, 1957, toward the end of Ruiz Cortines' period of office, a new committee was organized in Saragosa to work for construction of the dam, the Patronato Pro-Construcción de la Presa. Since one of its members was and remains a personal antagonist of the mayor who headed the previous commission, it was difficult to capture any continuity in the project. Besides this individual, who has long been the director of the local office of CANACINTRA, the other prominent members of the committee were a medical doctor, presently the head of the local Social Security Institute and a former municipal president (mayor F); the doctor who was also a participant in the boulevard affair and by reputation a local influential; another former mayor (mayor J) who was the owner of a mill and president of the local CANACINTRA; and the director of the local branch of the Banco Nacional de Crédito Ejidal.

Nothing else happened in the intervening period until a new President, Díaz Ordaz, and a new governor appeared on the scene. The governor was the same person who had created the urbanization plan for the state. Apparently the combination of a governor committed to obtaining the necessary funds to begin the construction, a President who agreed to the project, and the approval of a loan from the Inter-American Development Bank was sufficient to carry into operation the long-standing promise for a dam. A final element that at last seemed to make construction feasible was the overcoming of opposition from interests in the next state west which for years had fought the proposal on the grounds that a dam in this state would severely limit the flow of waters from the river into their state.

Just as the demands for a dam stemmed largely from the predominance of agricultural interests in the southeastern part of the state and thus bore a direct relationship to the prosperity of the city, so too there was a great deal of attention focused on the prevailing agricultural prices. While this matter was completely removed from local politics, this issue directly affected the community and was constantly discussed and in the news.

During the summer of 1966 there were a number of organizations and associations in Saragosa for the protection of agricultural inter-

31

ests. Among these were three financial institutions—the Unión de Crédito Agrícola y Ganadero, a cooperative association created to provide credit to small landowners engaged in agricultural and livestock production; the Banco Nacional de Crédito Agrícola, a governmental bank providing credit to small landholders; and the Banco Nacional de Crédito Ejidal, a government bank providing credit for the *ejiditarios* (those who worked communal lands). There were also three associations banding together agricultural interests—Agricultores y Ganaderos del ———, the Asociación de Agricultores del Río ———, and the Asociación de Avicultores. The first two of these associations were more general in character, while the last was a specialized group devoted to problems presented in the raising of chickens and the marketing of eggs at a free market rate.

While there was an extensive organizational framework through which local farming interests worked, none of this activity was focused at the community level. All of these organizations were national in character and their branches operating at a local level focused their attention on regional, state, and national organizations. Regardless of the fact that certain basic products such as beans, wheat, and corn were protected by national price controls and others of importance in the area, such as alfalfa and garlic, had to compete on an open market, there was little experience among local producers, *ejiditarios* and private landowners alike, in cooperating to ameliorate their conditions. While there were politics involved in such matters as selling prices and getting the producers to sell their products to processing plants or mills at an unfavorable rate for those cultivating the land, these matters were completely out of the range of attention of local authorities. However, this was a topic of interest to the PRI federal deputy for the district and was an issue on which the local PAN organization was trying to capitalize in the building of rural support. In the former case, the deputy had been active in trying to get the *ejiditarios* in his district to form an alfalfa cooperative so they could better protect their interests and not be subject to so much exploitation by those to whom they sold the alfalfa.

5. THE MUNICIPALITY
AS A POLITICAL
AND SOCIAL SUBSYSTEM

If one considers the ninefold typology that Wagley and Harris have developed of Latin American subcultures—Tribal Indian, Modern Indian, Peasant, Engenho Plantation, Usina Plantation, Town, Metropolitan Upper Class, Metropolitan Middle Class, and Urban Proletariat—there is little in contemporary political science literature on Latin America that makes any attempt to develop a comparable typology of political subsystems applicable to the area. Either we encounter a topical approach dealing with such subjects as the Latin American executive and Latin American political parties, or country-by-country analysis, devoted in the past to institutions and today to consideration of twenty independent political systems within the broad category of "developing areas." Yet recent developments in systems theory open up the region potentially to much more exacting analysis and provide us with a conceptual tool that can get at the linkage between communities, states or provinces, and national government more effectively. Just as we can single out typologies in the field of anthropology designed to capture the diversity of institutions, values, and behavioral patterns within the Latin American ethos, it is likewise relevant to look for variations in political style and behavior that cut across national boundaries.

This study is concerned with the analysis of a single community, conceived of as a political subsystem. If one superimposes Wagley and Harris' model of town subculture on this basis, we can situate the community in a larger comparative framework. The basic elements allowing us to define Saragosa as a town are the presence of two strongly contrasting subcultures—that of the town and the peasant—and the political and economic dominance of upper-class townsmen. Wagley and Harris observe that the contrast between the two subcultures "leads to marked schism in socioeconomic class status between a nonfarming, landlord, business-owning, bureaucratic, 'white-collar' group and a farming, manual-laboring group."

Within the town itself, there are a small number of people who are craft specialists, like shoemakers, blacksmiths, and carpenters, who are permanent residents of the town, and who do not engage in agricultural activities. From the point of view of the local upper-class these people may be "hicks" just as much as the town-dwelling and country-dwelling farmers. Although these artisans themselves often regard the rural people with condescension, the fact is that they are generally more closely related (by kinship, by marriage, by social and cultural values, by economics, and by social intercourse) with the rural farmers than with the town upper-class. The stigma of poverty, of illiteracy, and of manual labor is on both groups.[1]

The first thing that strikes the observer arriving in Saragosa is precisely this contrast between two very distinct subcultures. This is the reason population figures are misleading. An urban population of some 58,000 inhabitants, seen from the vantage point of the United States, would not readily lead one to think of such a community as a small town. But since by far the majority of Saragosa's inhabitants belong to a peasant subculture, they are not really participants in the urban life of the community. Their places of residence are strung along a seemingly endless number of muddy streets and theirs are the homes that lack such services as water, sewage disposal, and proper drainage.

In the period from 1953 to 1955, federal statistics reported the following conditions in Saragosa, on the basis of an urban population of 34,426. Of 6,500 places of residence, 33 per cent were considered substandard, 41.3 per cent lacked water, and 56 per cent were without drainage. While some of the streets were provided with a roadbed of stones of a sort, only 25 per cent were properly paved—in this case with concrete. These conditions have been aggravated by a substantial increase in urban population between 1940 and 1960. Prior to this, the city experienced little change. The 1921 census records an urban population of 24,035; the 1930 census, 24,480; the 1940 census, 22,421; the 1950 census, 34,424; and the 1960 census, 58,851.[2]

1. Charles Wagley and Marvin Harris, "A Typology of Latin American Subcultures," in Adams and Heath, p. 53.
2. México, Dirección General de Estadística, *VIII Censo General de Población, 1960; VII Censo General de Población, 1950; VI Censo de Población, 1940; V Censo de Población, 15 de Mayo de 1930; México, Departamento de la Estadística Nacional, Resumen del Censo General de Habitantes de 30 de Noviembre de 1921.*

One of the interview questions asked what socioeconomic changes the interviewee had been able to notice over the last thirty years. The general consensus was that in the past Saragosa was a closed community socially with a small upper class. Before the land reform era, which extended roughly from 1920 to 1936, this upper class was based on large landholdings. Since then it has depended on commercial activity. But regardless of this change in occupation and a complete turnover in the families making up the local socioeconomic elite, their style of living and value systems have remained almost identical. Their ideals remain those of the plantation gentry of another day and the gentleman complex is still very much alive.

An example of this change in the personages of the small upper class without a corresponding change in style of life is the family which was ranked number one on the basis of socioeconomic characteristics in every case where a response was obtainable. The founder of the family arrived in Saragosa around 1937 or 1938 and over the years he and his sons have built up an impressive complex of businesses. The first family operation was the establishment of a dealership in farm machinery representing Allis-Chalmers. From this they have branched out into a second dealership in farm equipment as the representatives for International Harvester. Other machinery is sold, such as General Electric diesel motors and Johnston water pumps, but the dealerships provide the focus for each operation. Additional family enterprises include commercial and industrial refrigeration, a consumer-goods store selling furniture and electrical appliances, a supermarket, and a beer distributorship. Complementing those activities in the city is an extensive farming operation centering around the cultivation of garlic. This likewise is a family endeavor, given present agrarian laws in Mexico. Legally a citizen may hold no more than one hundred hectares of arable land. Since the commercial production of garlic, to be profitable, requires a considerably larger land unit for cultivation, a solution was found through family cooperation. Each of four brothers owns one hundred hectares of land and this is complemented by an additional hundred hectares of rented land that is used for crop rotation. Given their resources and technical knowledge, the brothers have been able to work the land properly on an intensive basis. Joined to this is the fact that each brother has invested in one major piece of farm machinery which he shares with his brothers.

On looking at the commercial enterprises in Saragosa, one is struck not only by their number but also by the investments they represent. Using the yellow pages of the telephone book as a guide, there were, during the summer of 1966, sixteen firms specializing in the sale of farm machinery and miscellaneous equipment used in mechanized agriculture, nine automobile and truck agencies, two major wheat mills, fourteen furniture stores of which several also dealt in electrical appliances, five companies specializing in livestock feeds, seven firms engaged in the sale of commercial gas and gas appliances, two milk plants, three cold-drink bottling plants, three beer distributorships, and nine banks. Four of the banks were governmental institutions and three specialized in agricultural credit. None of them, however, was controlled by local capital; all were branches of national or regional banks. Finally, one of the concerns selling commercial gas and gas appliances represented a major investment in that the home office was located in Saragosa with branches in cities throughout the state and in the neighboring state capital.

In discussing the development of Saragosa as a commercial center for the region, many of the interviewees focused on subsequent changes in social structure. While there were a number of families who had amassed considerable wealth, they maintained that previous divisions between a small upper class and a large number of poor were no longer so marked and that a sizable middle class consisting of professionals—doctors, lawyers, and teachers primarily, bureaucratic officials in the employment of federal, state, and local governments, and "white collar" employees in various private enterprises—had emerged in Saragosa. Likewise they felt that the community was no longer so closed to outsiders as a consequence of its development as a regional commercial center. Many of the firms in operation during 1966 were established and owned by families who had come to Saragosa from elsewhere. Yet acceptance into the local upper class was conditioned by certain standards of behavior. While sufficient means were important, money alone did not qualify an individual for entrance into this small town elite. One individual, the owner of a local restaurant which was considered one of the few respectable places where the local elite could pass the hours, defined the differences in terms of the coincidence of money and Spanish lineage.

The need to diversify the economic bases of Saragosa, then, did not stem from the absence of money in the city, for there was considerable wealth in the hands of a number of families. The problem was the instability of the local economy because of its dependence on agricultural cycles in the valley. There was also the lack of an adequate number of jobs for the mass of the people. The growth of the city had come about largely through the influx of people identified with the peasant subculture of the surrounding region into the city. Given the conservative orientation of those with means and their general reluctance to participate in politics, the political leadership—even though it was drawn essentially from among local businessmen and professionals—found it necessary to look outside the community for a resolution of those problems.

Regardless of the small town atmosphere of Saragosa, there was a surprisingly large amount of group activity within the framework of formal organizations among those who participated in the town subculture. Each of these institutions comprised "a constellation or network of communication or influence."[3] An example of this activity may be seen in an unsuccessful attempt in May, 1965, to get the Ministry of Public Works to alter its decision to have a new toll road bypass the city and to locate the exit for the city some five kilometers north.[4] In this instance the local CANACINTRA office—not the political leadership—functioned as the primary communication and influence link among the various groupings. Besides the CANACINTRA office, those concerned were the municipal authorities; the local CANACO office; the Club de Leones; the Club Rotario; the Club 20-30; the Club Campestre, a local country club; the Mutualista Feminil, a women's club organized on a cooperative basis and supplying social services to the community; professional associations such as the Colegio Médico (doctors), the Colegio de Abogados y Notarios (lawyers and notary publics), and the Colegio de Contadores (public accountants); the Sociedad Mutualista "La Fraternal," a men's cooperative club providing medical insurance, loans, life insurance, and casino privileges for its members; Mujeres Pro-

3. William L. C. Wheaton, "Integration at the Urban Level: Political Influence and the Decision Process," in Philip E. Jacob and James V. Toscano (eds.), *The Integration of Political Communities* (Philadelphia: J. B. Lippincott Company, 1964), p. 124.

4. This issue was not selected for decision-making analysis because of the paucity of information. Within the course of the interviews this topic was raised at random intervals, but to no avail. For all concerned it was of secondary importance.

fesionistas y de Negocios (Business and Professional Women); and the local tourist department. These associations were joined by four local plants, the petrochemical company, the fertilizer firm, a local canning factory, and one of the two large wheat mills, and several unions—the local office of the Federación Regional de Obreros y Campesinos, the Unión de Productores de Cajeta, the Unión de Tablajeros, and the Unión de Cantineros.

Besides these formal organizations there were a number of labor associations and *ad hoc* groups devoted to particular issues. The best example of *ad hoc* group activity is the school issue. No less than nine commissions and associations appeared at the time of the conflict. Likewise in the boulevard issue the protest movement was initiated and given momentum by an *ad hoc* organization.

On the other hand, up through 1966 Saragosa had had little or no experience in developing civic betterment boards (Juntas de Mejoramiento Moral, Cívico y Material) of the sort described by Marvin Alisky.[5] Neither did the city maintain a Patronato de Educación, a parent-teacher type association present in other Mexican states. There were, however, a Patronato de Bomberos (devoted to raising funds for the local fire department), a Patronato de la Cruz Roja (the Red Cross), and a Comité de Acción Cívica y Social (a committee established by the municipal authorities to handle public holidays, commemorations, and other civic affairs).

Prior to 1942 politics in Saragosa was personalistic and unstable and social organizations of the sort just described were few or nonexistent. The major political fact facing Saragosa was the implementation of the national government's agrarian reform program. What vestiges remained of the local landowning elite disappeared rapidly. The men imposed by the governor on the community as municipal presidents were the governor's men, and they came not from the old elite but from among the groups that had identified themselves with the Revolution.

The municipal archives before 1942 record a constant turnover in local governmental personnel and frequent intervention in community affairs by the state government. The last two mayors before 1942 symbolize this leadership: one was an *ejiditario*, the other a man from the *pueblo* who earned his living in the production of *cajeta*, a local caramel-type sweet made from goat's milk.

Beginning in 1942 a new era in the type of local leadership en-

5. Alisky, "Mexico's Special Districts: Municipal Civic Betterment Boards."

sued, lasting through 1963. During this period mayors in Saragosa were selected from among the new upper class—small-town businessmen and professionals. Certainly the governor continued to exercise his prerogative in indicating who would be the local PRI candidate and, in a one-party setting, this insured his election. Nevertheless, a real attempt was made to select men who were acceptable to the community's upper sector.[6] None of the eight mayors was forcibly removed; all were duly elected and served out their periods of office.

There was only one case after 1942 of a governor directly intervening in municipal affairs. This came about, however, not because of a misunderstanding with the governor but because the governor himself was removed by the President, in January, 1946. A newly elected town council assumed office on the first of January and on the seventh, federal intervention in the state capital took place. The members of the council were removed from office, but the municipal president (mayor H) was allowed to remain and, with the consent of the new governor, to name a Junta de Administración Civil which functioned as his council for the remainder of his term.

In all of the interviews where a direct answer could be obtained, the interviewees agreed that significant changes had taken place in community leadership. They referred to the 1930's as an era in Saragosa of continual conflict between the *sinarquistas,* a radical Church-oriented group, and the *agraristas,* the revolutionary agrarian elements identified with the new order. Beginning about 1940 as divisions within the community began to subside, a shift took place within the local PRI. Hitherto, the agrarian sector of the party had apparently predominated. The balance of power then passed to the popular sector and a real attempt was made to co-opt the community's economic leaders into the party structure.

This preeminence of the popular sector is reflected not only in the mayors but also in the council members. For example, the incumbent mayor, at the time the interviewing was carried out, had a

6. Throughout the remainder of this study the terms "upper sector" and "lower sector" will be used in accordance with the work of Richard N. Adams ("Introduction" in Richard N. Adams and Dwight B. Heath [eds.], *Contemporary Cultures and Societies of Latin America,* pp. 266-70). In Saragosa political influence was the monopoly of the upper sector after 1941. These divisions, which refer to the use of political power, correspond to the existence of two distinct subcultures (one town, the other peasant) in terms of social structure.

council consisting of five representatives drawn from the popular sector. Three were prosperous local businessmen, one a medical doctor, and the other a PRI party functionary who was jointly secretary-general of CNOP (the popular sector) and the *suplente* (the elected substitute) for the PRI federal deputy from Saragosa. Three *regidores* came from the other two sectors, one representing the agrarian sector, and two the worker sector. Yet only one of the labor sector representatives—a former official in the local electrical union —really could be classified as working class; the second certainly belonged in the lower reaches of the community's upper sector. Although he was the leader of the local railroad union, he was a ticket agent, the owner of a small farm, and held stock along with fifty-two other associates in a local trucking company.

6. POLITICAL FACTIONS

Beginning in 1961 fissures appeared in the community's power structure. Prior to that date there was no question that the local PRI had absorbed into its ranks all important local groups and was performing quite well its role as an aggregator of interests. But since then several developments have coincided which may eventually push Saragosa in the direction of competitive politics and bring about an increase in citizen political participation.

From 1942 to 1961 the mayors of Saragosa were men drawn from private life whose primary interests were non-political. The prevailing pattern was for the governor of the state to indicate from among several potential candidates the person of his choice. Considerable care was taken to see that the mayor-elect was acceptable not only to the governor and to the PRI (his papers were always sent to Mexico City to be approved) but also to local business and professional interests. Once agreement had been reached behind the scenes as to who would be the next candidate, the individual would proceed to line up votes in each of the three sectors. The convention of the local PRI was then held; a number of persons would be nominated from the floor, among them the governor's choice; votes would be cast; and the semi-official candidate, his name now revealed to the public, would emerge victorious. This was followed by the general election where as the only candidate he would win automatically. On the first of the year he would be installed as the city's next municipal president. After a period of office extending for two years until 1951 and three years since, and an uneventful reign in which he would devote himself to what were essentially administrative tasks, he would step down and return to private business. A few of these former mayors would retain their political ties, but by far the majority would engage in no further political activity.

In contrast, the last two mayors (in the time span extending from 1942 through 1966) maintained political expectations and the hope of using their position as the beginning of political careers. This was less true of mayor B, whose period of office extended from 1961 through 1963. He was essentially a transitional type. As a local businessman and member of the most prominent local political family, he had a foot in both camps, so to speak. About mayor A (1964-66) there can be no doubt. The crisis over the boulevard revealed his position essentially as that of a politician tied to the coattails of the governor, with political aspirations of his own, and without support from a sizable portion of the town's business community. Whether or not this will remain the pattern is yet to be seen, for at the time of the interviews the men receiving the closest attention from the governor for the next term of office, since the November convention of the local PRI was approaching, were three prominent local businessmen (two of whom were presently on the town council) and the former state deputy.

This situation whereby a change in the style of community leadership seemed to be under way was joined to a second development: a shift in the internal power structure of the local PRI, independent of sector lines, as one faction replaced another.

Apparently, ever since the institutionalization of the Revolutionary Party in the state at large, there have been two major factions, the *rojos* (Reds) and the *verdes* (Greens). Those who were willing to talk about these factions stressed the fact that this terminology did not reflect ideological or sector divisions. The names, they said, came from colors in the Mexican flag and in the PRI's party emblem and defined two distinct groups based on close personal ties extending throughout the state and up to the level of national politics. Fluctuations in community factional control are summarized in the following chart.

MAYORS AND RULING FACTIONS (1942-1966)

Year	Mayor Identifi- cation Symbol	Faction Represented by Municipal President
1964-66	A	Verde
1961-63	B	Rojo/Verde
1958-60	C	Rojo
1955-57	D	Rojo
1952-54	E	Rojo
1950-51	F	Rojo
1948-49	G	Rojo
1946-47	H	Verde/Rojo
1944-45	I	Verde
1942-43	J	Verde

In the interviews it was impossible to identify any stable faction before 1942. The terminology *rojo* and *verde* appeared only to become meaningful in Saragosa after 1942 when business and professional leadership in the community became the established pattern. This does not mean these factions did not exist before this date, for mayor C stated that these informal divisions had existed in the state party ever since he could remember and that they were simply a part of the prevailing order. What they suggest is the existence of an internal communication and influence network, providing links with political elites, built on the basis of close personal relationships. Shifts in the preeminence of one group or the other in Saragosa have coincided with changes in the person of the governor.

Both groups, whether currently in favor or not, have provided for political representation at the national level. In recent years this representation has been supplied primarily by four men who, because of their preeminence in state politics and reputations extending beyond the regional level, were accredited by local influentials with access to the "Revolutionary Family's inner circle."[1] The two *rojos* were former state governors. One was state governor for the period 1955-60, while the other, besides serving as governor in 1933, was a federal deputy and for a short time president of the PRI. This part of his political career ended with the accession of Lázaro Cárdenas to the presidency in 1934; as a *callista* he went into exile. Later he returned to government and filled administrative posts. The two *verdes* were also former state governors who held office, prior to the era of *rojo* domination in the state, during the presidency of Cárdenas. One of these men had had quite an illustrious political career. Beginning as a postal employee in Saragosa, he became a deputy in the state legislature and from there went on to become a federal deputy. After serving as governor of the state, he held administrative posts as a subsecretary in the Ministry of Interior (Gobernación) and as an executive (*jefe*) in the Ministry of Labor (Departamento del Trabajo). He was also active as a journalist, was an owner of a major paper company in the Federal District, and the father of the federal deputy (in 1966) for the PRI from Saragosa. The other, after a long era of political prominence in

1. In conceptualizing the network of relationships extending upward and outward from Saragosa, the most useful model of Mexico's governing elite encountered was that provided by Frank R. Brandenburg. In *The Making of Modern Mexico*, Brandenburg refers to the governing elite as "the Revolutionary Family" and divides it into three levels: an "inner council" at the top, a second level occupied by those on the fringes of power, and "the formal political apparatus" (pp. 4-5).

the state, was approaching senility. At the time of the interviewing, the repesentation of *verde* interests had been weakened by the aging of these two political influentials and the blowup over the governor's urbanization plan. As of the summer of 1966 both the PRI deputy from Saragosa and his father were spending the majority of their time in Mexico City.

The exact way in which these relationships functioned over the twenty-five-year period extending from 1942 through 1966 could not be determined on the basis of the interviews, yet the broad patterns are clear. First, the switch from the predominance of the *verdes* to the *rojos* in 1946 appears to be the result of federal intervention in state politics, following disturbances and demonstrations in the state's major city, and the removal of the incumbent governor. Municipal president H (who has since died) had only been in office some six days when these events took place. According to a close friend of his who served as one of his *regidores*, he was allowed to remain in office through the intercession of the first of two federal interventors, a man who happened to be a friend of both the mayor and the *regidor* and was willing to attest to the mayor's honesty and character. The mayor had an additional asset in his favor. He was well thought of locally and acceptable to both factions. For this reason, the mayor for the two-year term extending from January 1, 1946, through December 31, 1947, has been identified as a *verde/rojo*. Depending on the individual interviewed, there was disagreement as to which of the two factions he favored or was favored by; some placed an emphasis on the *verdes*, others on the *rojos*.

Between 1947 and 1960, relationships between the governor and the local political elite remained stable. The governor for the term extending from September 26, 1949, to September 26, 1955, was a *rojo*, as was the next governor, whose incumbency covered the next six-year period. Likewise, in Saragosa each of the five mayors in office during these years belonged to the *rojo* faction and all had in common the fact that as businessmen (this applied to three) or professionals (the other two), none of them really had any interest in politics. Their administrations were honest, a little on the dull side, and non-controversial. Theirs were essentially caretaker governments reflecting the new status quo.

By 1961, a change had taken place in state politics. The new governor, according to the interviewees, was a *verde* and committed to instituting a development plan for the state as a whole to bring it "into the twentieth century." A corresponding shift took place in Saragosa. The *rojos*, who had established themselves as the major group in the local PRI, were now on the outs. Into their former position of favor the *verdes* now moved. Their distinguishing characteristics were commitment to the dynamic leadership of the new state government and the desire to get things moving in the municipality. Whereas the former *rojo* mayors maintained no interest in politics and saw their function primarily in terms of letting business go on in the community as usual, the succeeding two mayors (A and B) developed programs designed to institute improvements in the municipality.

There is some doubt as to whether mayor B can be classified as a *verde* or a *rojo*. His predecessor, mayor C, was emphatic in identifying him with his faction, while a prominent local businessman, who was related to a former governor identified with the *verde* group and who had a son-in-law in the new state government, was equally insistent that he was a *verde*. Earlier it was stated that the data collected identified him with both factions. A further factor suggesting this interpretation is that mayor B was the son of mayor H, a man who had pursued the same policy of identifying himself with both groups, and was a member of a politically active family. One wing of the family had maintained allegiance to the PRI while the other—still participating jointly in family enterprises—had passed into the PAN. As of the end of 1966, this family had provided three municipal presidents (mayors H, E, and B) and the district's first federal deputy for PAN. The PAN deputy was the brother of mayors H and E and the uncle of mayor B.

Mayor B developed a program while he was in office committed to the improvement of the surrounding rural areas in the *municipio* through expanded health services and schooling. He likewise devoted considerable attention to attracting new firms to Saragosa, when the opportunity presented itself, and familiarized himself with municipal government practices in the United States.

Mayor A abandoned this concern for the rural areas for active participation in the governor's state-wide urbanization plan. Not only did he work to facilitate execution of this plan in the municipality, he also established a committee, consisting of three prominent businessmen who were serving as *regidores*, devoted to amassing basic statistics and information of the sort that could be used to attract new companies. In addition, he proceeded to reorganize and upgrade municipal administration so that the demands of the community could be processed on a more rational basis.

The third development pushing Saragosa in the direction of a more amorphous power structure—congruent with greater differentiation within the socioeconomic structure of the community's upper sector—was the creation of an opposition party, the PAN—conservative in its orientation and attractive to the well-to-do. The consequence of this development was a three-way division in politically oriented business and professional groups. Boundaries, however, were not clear-cut because PAN's growth in Saragosa had been based on an appeal to the community's electorate at the level of national elections only—either for President or for representatives to the national congress. Apparently many people identified with the PRI and voting the PRI ticket in local and state elections were casting their ballots for the PAN candidate during national elections. However, the extent to which PAN represented a major force in the community could not be determined precisely since, regardless of many attempts to obtain electoral statistics from the state capital and many polite assurances as to their availability, the researcher was unable to gain access to such data.

The interview material, however, does suggest some guidelines as to PAN action in the community. First, several of the people interviewed defined themselves as PRI regulars in state and local elections because there was no effective choice (nor could there be under present arrangements) and as sympathetic to PAN at the time of national elections. Second, the PRI federal deputy considered the PAN as a major force in the Saragosa district. He stated that this had made reorganization of the state party essential since, for the first time, it was up against an organized opposition. Third, the PAN deputy and his *suplente* claimed that they had actually won the election. While the PRI deputy disagreed with this assertion, he did state that he had won the election by only a slight margin. Fourth, both the PAN deputy and his *suplente,* as well as many others interviewed, stressed the attempt by PAN in Saragosa to function as a "loyal opposition" and to develop a broader appeal based on moderate reform and a disassociation from the party's previous reputation for being "tied to the skirts of the clergy." Yet none of them felt that PAN stood any real chance of emerging as a major party. They believed that the road ahead was full of many obstacles, that they could not expect to participate fully at the local level without inviting intervention by the governor, and that their best strategy was to build a solid foundation and to exert pressure in such a way that it would force the local PRI to function more in accord with the democratic norms built into its party statutes—and to wait for the right opportunity.

7. THE FINDINGS

At the outset, three independent variables and an intervening variable were isolated to see if they could establish a relationship with the object of this study: the inclusiveness or exclusiveness of the decision-making structure of a Mexican community. While in the real world these factors are intertwined, they were singled out for analytical purposes to see if they could provide a more systematic way of looking at this aspect of politics.

There seems to be a close correlation between the decision-making structure and the economic structure of Saragosa. As indicated previously, the community fits Wagley and Harris' town typology closely. There is a sharp division between a small group of townsmen engaged in non-farming, landlord, business-owning, bureaucratic, and "white-collar" activities, and a majority who can be classified as participants in a peasant subculture. Prior to 1942 political leadership came from the lower sector; since that date it has come from the upper sector. Yet, while there has been a change in the socioeconomic background of the local political elite, the PRI in Saragosa as an organization-in-the-electorate still bases its strength on the town's lower sector and the residents of the surrounding rural area.

This pattern of politics by and large parallels what Donald Brand described in his study of Quiroga, Michoacán, in 1945.[1] In this instance the factor of size does not seem to represent an important variable since Quiroga at the time of the study had a total population of 8,672 in the *municipio* and only 3,161 inhabitants in the town proper. Brand observed that while the local PRI was divided into the same three sectors as the national party, the major division in the community was between town and country, the well-to-do and the poor, the white and the Indian, the landed and the landless or *ejiditario*, the Church-oriented *sinarquistas* and the agrarian radicals.[2] Although Saragosa is located in another state and does not have a distinct Indian population, similar divisions exist within the community. Today, however, the antipathies between the *sinarquistas* and the *agaristas* have disappeared from the scene in Saragosa. Also, since a substantial segment of Saragosa's urban population be-

1. Donald D. Brand, *Quiroga: A Mexican Municipio*, p. 102.
2. *Ibid.*, p. 104.

longs to a peasant subculture, the town-country dichotomy is not nearly so clear-cut.

There is also a parallel in the alternations in community leadership. Brand states that in the period extending from 1917 to 1934, the equivalent of the present popular sector controlled the *ayuntamiento*. This was followed by a period of turmoil lasting from 1934 to 1938, during which the state government imposed the town council. Then, from 1938 to 1945, the peasant sector was dominant, although the other two sectors did receive representation on the council. In 1946, the popular sector returned to power. In 1947, PAN won control of the town council and, as might be expected, intervention by the state governor resulted.[3]

Prior to 1933, no information was collected in Saragosa other than general references, and between 1933 and 1938, material available in the municipal archives is sketchy. What it does reveal, though, is a constant change in mayor as the state governor repeatedly intervened in local affairs. This pattern, which is much clearer after 1938, continued until 1940. These years of lower-sector rule were ones of turmoil, similar to those described by Brand for the period from 1934 to 1938. The only period of stability occurred between 1940 and 1942. This was an administration, however, in which the three commissions of *hacienda* (municipal finances), *aguas potables y salubridad* (public health and water supply), and *jardines y parques* (municipal parks and gardens) were held by *regidores* representing the popular sector and belonging to the town's subculture.

Quiroga's experience with the PAN has not been reproduced in Saragosa due to the flexibility of the local PRI structure and to a movement from imposition of municipal presidents by the governor to a process of co-optation whereby individuals from the business-professional group were brought into positions of leadership. Also, when PAN finally did emerge as an opposition party in the community, it did not seek to win control of local government.

This preeminence of business and professional interests in Saragosa confirms some of the findings of D'Antonio and associates in their studies of Ciudad Juárez and Tijuana as well as those of Klapp and Padgett in their study of Tijuana.[4] In each case the au-

3. *Ibid.*, pp. 104-5.
4. William V. D'Antonio, William H. Form, Charles P. Loomis, and Eugene C. Erickson, "Institutional and Occupational Representation in Eleven Com-

thors found the local elite to be composed mainly of businessmen. Nevertheless, those findings differ from the conclusions of this study when it comes to a discussion of the handling of political power. In each case the findings show a substantial gap between business interests and the governmental leadership provided by the PRI at the community level. The explanation for this variation is to be found not so much in contrasting economic structure and distance from the border with the United States (as the investigators suggested) as it is in the handling of political skills by economic groups in these communities.

A further modification of these authors' findings is the grouping in this study of business and professional interests into substantially one category, termed the upper sector or the town subculture. The explanation here suggests that this variation is to be justified according to the size of the community studied. While Ciudad Juárez and Tijuana are cities with populations of 250,000 and 160,000 respectively, Saragosa is a city of some 58,000. Leaving aside these differences, the distribution of power is similar in each of these communities. There is no single group that runs things due to the prevalence of personal factions within each of these local elites and different networks for contact and communication built on personal relationships.

The second independent variable—the extent of extra-community control over economic groups in the community—also suggests a correlation with the nature of the local decision-making structure. The political leaders selected from the business-professional group were long-time residents of Saragosa whose financial resources came from within the community. Officials employed by local banks—that is, in enterprises whose control comes from sources external to the community—as well as the management of the new firms which have come into the area recently, have avoided participation in local politics.

Between 1942 and 1963 there was an overlapping of political and economic leadership in the person of the mayor and the members of the town council. This meant that there was considerable contact between these two groups. Yet, by and large, when communication

munity Influence Systems"; William V. D'Antonio and William H. Form, *Influentials in Two Border Cities: A Study in Community Decision-Making*; Orrin E. Klapp and L. Vincent Padgett, "Power Structure and Decision-Making in a Mexican Border City."

took place, it was carried on informally and never in public. There is always the possibility that these relationships might change, but this is a question of external political controls and the use of political skills. It may be that 1964 marks the beginning of a pattern which will reproduce the findings of the border city studies—of a substantial gap between businessmen and local political leaders. This, however, leads into a consideration of the third independent variable.

In the Mexican case there can be no doubt as to the importance of extra-community political control over the resolution of local issues, due to the centralized nature of the political system. This study confirms what is already general knowledge regarding the distribution of political power in Mexico. While attention has been focused more on state government than on national government, this is justified in a sense because the selection of mayors in the municipality across the years studied has borne a direct relationship to the person of the governor.

Nevertheless, this distribution of political power should never be construed to imply necessarily an authoritarian arrangement nor a dichotomy between political and business interests. There is ample room for variation. Two patterns of power are now apparent: the first consists of a sharp division between political leadership and the local business elite; the second reflects integration of political and economic leadership.

In Saragosa the governor's control over the *municipio* has shifted from imposition to co-optation. As a consequence, with the exception of two incidents—one in 1946 and the other in November, 1964 —government in Saragosa has remained stable over the last twenty-five years. The key to this arrangement has been the acceptance on the part of the local elite of a political order dominated by a single party and of the primacy of the governor in state politics. On the part of the various governors it has depended upon their ability to retain close ties with individuals in the community's upper sector who are respected by their fellow townsmen. All concerned recognize that the governor must be assured of municipal presidents on whom he can rely. Otherwise, under the present system, he could not function effectively as the state's chief executive and carry out his programs. At the same time all governors in recent history have been careful to enter into close consultation with local influentials. Before indicating their preferences, they have checked out the potential candidate's standing with business and professional interests. But given the variety of personal networks existing within the community, continuity in leadership has never meant that any one single group has dominated the municipality successfully.

During his period of office the municipal president is supreme in local affairs. He is the community's political leader in every respect; he is the official to whom all citizens turn when they desire services or wish to have a situation corrected; and he is the community's chief broker and representative within the state political system. Yet the prestige that he acquires is the prestige of office, for once he steps down he returns to private life and does not necessarily continue to take an active role in local politics. This interpretation of the municipal president as the single most important local political figure is based on existing local government literature in Mexico, on the role of the mayor in the first three issues examined in this study, and on the results of the interview material.

An example of the mayor's preeminence is reflected in the formulation of the annual budget. Before submitting it to the state legislature for approval, the mayor is required by federal law to consult with a committee formed from CANACO and CANACINTRA members.[5] In practice it was found that whether this process of consultation was used or not depended on the discretion of the mayor. Some of the mayors, particularly at an earlier date, used this structure as a way of always obtaining consensus from local business interests. Others, in particular mayor A, simply bypassed the procedure and the decision was made by the municipal president in consultation with the *regidor* in charge of *hacienda* and the municipal treasurer. During mayor A's administration this method of deciding on the annual budget almost exclusively with the advice of selected council members was a further element in the growing estrangement between a substantial part of local business interests and the community's political leadership. On the other hand, the *regidor* exercising the commission in *hacienda* was a member of the most prominent local family, in terms of socioeconomic background, and a successful businessman in his own right. So it could well be that the same process of consultation with local businessmen over the budget was continuing—only that it now was following a much

5. This law is included in "Leyes de la Cámera de Comercio y Cámeras de Industria en Transformación en Vigor" of May 2, 1941, and published in the *Diario Oficial* of August 26, 1941.

more informal path and thus was subjected more to the particular network of personal relationships maintained by the incumbent mayor.

Once again, these findings support those of D'Antonio and Form in their study of Ciudad Juárez, particularly in their identification of the prestige of the mayor more with the office than with the person.

Although the voting for the Juárez mayor approached unanimity, his influence was said to be conditional upon occupying the office. Thus, while he held office, [he] could derive power from it which he could use either to his own personal advantage, or to making major community decisions, or both . . . [But the mayor] appeared to have power only to the extent that the governor was not interested.[6]

It now appears that the occupancy of a particular office is a prime requisite for power in Mexico, and this office is secured through PRI. To occupy office is to have both authority and influence, and these diminish as one descends the political ladder. From this point of view of the individual, the office limits both his power and influence.[7]

On the other hand, while D'Antonio and Form singled out changes between 1955 and 1958 leading in the direction of increased autonomy of the mayor from the governor and movement toward closer ties between business and politics as new departures, this was not the case in Saragosa. D'Antonio and Form related these developments to the emergence of a new type of mayor who was able to gain control of the local PRI without having served the party long and faithfully.[8] In contrast, from the Saragosa perspective, the presence of mayors who had not necessarily served the party long and faithfully and the closeness of business and politics was a part of the stable politics developed in the community since 1942.

To explain these differences, attention must be turned to this study's intervening variable: the political skills of the economic groups in the community. By now it should be apparent that those who have a monopoly on political skills in Saragosa by and large come from the upper sector. This does not mean that every person

6. D'Antonio and Form, pp. 77-78.
7. Ibid.
8. Ibid., pp. 121, 125.

within this group is politically motivated. As a matter of fact, by far the majority is apathetic. These citizens prefer to utilize their resources to pursue their immediate business and professional interests and to cultivate the art of leisure.

The limited distribution of political skills in Saragosa is demonstrated by the fact that only two municipal presidents in the period studied, mayors J and I, apparently had retained any political influence and this they exercised from behind the scenes. The exact pattern, however, is not clear, for if we re-examine the chart of political factions in Saragosa we find that these two mayors were identified with the *verde* faction, a group in ascendancy since 1961, and the incumbent governor.

It could be that one of the characteristics of the *rojo* faction was a particular style of gubernatorial leadership demonstrating a preference for caretaker mayors, for men who would show little interest in state politics. In every case the *rojo* mayors returned to private business at the end of their term of office, expressed little interest in politics, and conceived of the functions of local government as very limited. Joined with this perception was a second: They saw their administrations as "the providers of life's amenities" and as contributors to preserving the community's way of life. In contrast, the last two municipal presidents in the time span studied, mayors A and B, attempted to create administrations which would serve as instruments of community growth. Examples of this attitude were the interest of both mayors in obtaining new sources of income for the city, mayor B's interest in improving rural living conditions through inaugurating a public health program and expanding school services, and mayor A's reorganization of municipal administration so as to provide improved public services and his interest in obtaining benefits for Saragosa from the governor's urbanization plan.[9]

On the other hand, the absence of *rojo* participation in local politics at the time interviewing was carried out could represent recognition on their part that since their faction was on the outs, it did them little good to pursue political activities. The only way of veri-

9. This discussion of the perception of local government functions in terms of providing life's amenities, supplying caretaker administrations, and serving as instruments of community growth is based on the typology developed by Oliver Williams for the comparative study of local government, and on the discussion of this typology in Banfield and Wilson's *City Politics* (Oliver Williams, "A Typology for Comparative Local Government"; Banfield and Wilson, pp. 53-56).

fying this would be to wait for a period when a governor identified with the *rojos* would return to office.

One final dimension related to this discussion is the degree of pluralism or elitism in the community—that is, the extent to which power was concentrated or dispersed in Saragosa during the time span studied.

Regardless of upper sector control since 1942 and similarities in background and outlook among local political leaders, a cohesive power structure did not develop. Instead, what emerged in a town where anyone of importance knew everyone else of importance was a struggle for status among competing business-professional factions. This situation fit the desires of the various governors, for they wished to maintain their dominance over the *municipio* while, at the same time, doing this on the basis of co-optation rather than compulsion. Hence the shifting support of the governor from one faction to another within the business-professional group provided stability without allowing a competing power center to develop which might at some time present the governor with a situation difficult to control.

In speaking of factions in Saragosa it is important to distinguish between two distinct types: those based on a network of personal relationships and *confianza*; and those which took on the character of organized political factions within the local PRI, the *rojos* and the *verdes*. The first type of faction merits further discussion. Life among the upper sector in Saragosa focuses around a series of "relatively closed, completely informal primary group(s), held together in common interest by personal ties and including a roster of . . . key socio-politico-economic positions."[10] These informal organizations pervade the social, economic, and political life of the town's upper sector. While this phenomenon has been singled out by Leeds as a characteristic of Brazilian society and he refers to it as the *panelinha*, it is much more widespread throughout the various Latin American republics than his discussion would lead one to believe. The term *pandilla* will be used here to describe these relationships.

What exists in Saragosa is a factional style of politics, monopolized by the upper sector, operating within the framework of a democratic regime. Since 1942 there has been no challenge to busi-

10. Anthony Leeds, "Brazilian Careers and Social Structure: A Case History and Model," Adams and Heath, p. 387.

ness-professional leadership from the lower sector, either in the city or in the countryside. A system of relationships has developed in which the electorate in principle selects public officials. In form, power is distributed in such a way that equal weight is given to the three sectors represented in the local PRI. In reality the worker and the peasant sectors have accepted elite leadership as proper and just.[11]

The keystone of this arrangement for the sharing of political power with the state governor is the limited nature of political participation in the local political process. Certainly the mayor was always present when an issue arose requiring attention, but aside from him there were no others whose participation was deemed essential—at least visibly. The five issues examined support this more general finding. No more than a handful of men was ever really involved in the decision that was taken. And of these only the PAN deputy and the former medical doctor were involved in more than one issue.

This point is an important one in reconciling the existence of numerous social *pandillas* with the presence of two political factions. In an urban community such as Saragosa these solidarity groupings involved different relationships. The *pandillas* were essentially horizontal in structure, while the political factions were vertical, binding together individuals with different social status and reaching down into the lower sector. They were primarily communication and mobility networks. Furthermore, the two political factions did not seem to reflect the same degree of cohesiveness. While the *verde* faction apparently consisted of a more tightly knit group, the *rojos* were a loose coalition of *pandillas*, lacking a well-developed communication network reaching the lower sector. The contrast between these two groups was most clearly expressed by a council member in mayor A's administration. When the question was raised as to whether there was any one person or group who ran the city, his response was affirmative. This group, he said, was the *grupo verde*. It is not fitting for us to have people of any other sort ("*No*

11. A good example of this attitude is to be found in the comments of a labor union representative who during 1966 held a position on the council as a *regidor*. The issues raised in the interview and the responses that he gave were stated clearly in terms of what "they" did and the explanations "they" gave him as to what had been decided. Even though his position as a labor official and as a representative on the council for labor put him into close contact with community leaders, he was peripheral to the local decision-making process.

nos conviene tener gente de otra indole"), since for a number of years now the dominant group within the PRI has been the *grupo verde*. According to him, the term *rojo* had never really been used by those in the opposing group, rather it was a term employed by those calling themselves the *verdes*. While he did definitely perceive the existence of a *verde* faction, the *rojos* for him were an amorphous entity lacking much organization. But, it should be added, the *verdes* were not without their difficulties since included within their group were individuals sympathetic both to the business-professional interests of the local upper sector and to the needs of the peasants in the surrounding rural areas.

The one factor that was always crucial to how an issue was handled was the reaction of the governor. In a very real sense he and his administration determined the scope of government in relation to the economic and social systems of the community. What local autonomy existed in terms of a community political process depended on his person.

From 1942 through 1966 the scope of government in Saragosa remained limited. But this should not be taken to mean that there was a dearth of leadership skills in the city. There was a substantial pool of local talent within community social and economic organizations which could be tapped when necessary. This was precisely what was done when the time came to select a new mayor. In this respect the study confirms a finding of Klapp and Padgett in their analysis of Tijuana politics: "Much of the leadership of this community is outside governmental institutions, operating through civic associations, labor organizations, and *ad hoc juntas* or committees. Much is informal, working through cliques, friendships, and personal connections. Much is not public, except in stages where community support is desired to resolve a conflict or provide funds; generally speaking, the citizens at large do not make major decisions. [Yet] this does not mean that power is monolithic or hierarchic, in that a single group runs things."[12] In their study they found, just as in this case, that there were many key decisions made outside the community and that where local decisions were involved the elite was poorly integrated and not very powerful.

This pattern of power, however, is not peculiar to Mexico, for there are studies of North American communities demonstrating similar patterns. For example, what D'Antonio and Form observed

12. Klapp and Padgett, p. 405.

concerning El Paso, Texas, could well be applied to Saragosa: "It is possible to discern an evolutionary development in the structure of decision-making as communities move away from a pattern of landed aristocracy to industrialization. . . .

"Thus pluralism emerges in the American community when the business-professional groups are successfully challenged by the working class and ethnic groups. Until that occurs, much of what may pass as pluralism may be nothing but a struggle for status among competing business-professional factions, such as Hunter apparently found in Regional City."[13]

Finally, this study substantially confirms the secondary propositions submitted for examination at the beginning regarding the relationship between leadership patterns and the degree of citizen participation in local issues. While community leaders neither had access to the financial and economic resources of local banks and corporations, mentioned in the Presthus study, nor included bankers in their ranks, as indicated in Kammerer's *Urban Political Community*, they were quite clearly drawn from a business-professional elite. The only exception was mayor A, but the chances are that this was a temporary situation and that his isolation from a major part of the city's business leadership was brought about substantially by the boulevard affair. Even then he was, after all, a lawyer by profession and continued to draw his support from an important segment of the community's upper sector. For him to maintain his position, popular support was not essential.

This study also confirms Presthus' suggestion of a correlation between more centralized control and action by a few hyperactive leaders on the one hand, and poor social integration on the other. Not only was the community divided between upper and lower sectors, but also within the upper sector there was little integration. Added to this was the importance of the governor and the continued policies of state administrations in using *pandillas* in the upper sector to supply community leadership in such a way as to avoid creating a cohesive power structure.

13. D'Antonio and Form, pp. 230-31.

CONCLUDING REMARKS

By now the question of who governs in Saragosa has been answered substantially. But what does this mean and, if we are to attempt to take a comparative approach to the study of local government, where can we situate Saragosa? One possibility for classification is supplied by the typologies developed by Agger, Goldrich, and Swanson for the analysis of variations in power structure and types of regime.

In the case of their power structure syndrome, the use of two variables—distribution of political power among citizens and political leadership ideology—leads to four possible combinations: Consensual Mass, Consensual Elite, Competitive Mass, and Competitive Elite. If their definitions are strictly adhered to, Saragosa's power structure may be described as Consensual Elite, for one encounters a narrow distribution of political power among citizens and a political leadership ideology which is convergent. The important distinction to remember, if this classification scheme is used, is that "in the absence of ideological conflict among the political leaders, the power structure is classified as consensual no matter how conflicting the interest-group politics may be."[1] However, for our purposes it is not sufficient to think in terms of only one type of Consensual Elite, since Saragosa did not develop a cohesive power structure over the twenty-five years studied. Within the ideological framework provided by the Revolutionary Myth and cultivated by the PRI, a factional style of politics developed as a consequence of external and internal factors, i.e., the need by the governors of the state to maintain control over politics within the community which led to their desire not to have a cohesive power structure develop, and the presence of *pandillas* within the upper sector and poor integration among these groups.

If we apply the typology for regimes we find four possibilities emerging from the use of two variables: probability of illegitimate sanctions blocking efforts to shift the scope of government and sense of electoral potency. These are Developed Democracy, Guided Democracy, Underdeveloped Democracy, and Oligarchy. In these terms the regime existing in Saragosa is oligarchic, since

1. Agger, Goldrich, and Swanson, p. 116.

not only was there a low sense of electoral potency but also a high probability of illegitimate sanctions being applied to block any efforts to shift the scope of government. In so classifying Saragosa we must be aware of the particular definition given by Agger, Goldrich, and Swanson to the term "regime." They define regime as "the 'rules of the game' in political decision-making as political leaders in a polity conform to and interpret them."[2] To make this definition meaningful in the Mexican setting we must draw a distinction between the formalistic rules of the game and those that were actually put into practice during the time span studied. This is because in Saragosa there was a considerable discrepancy between democratic norms (expressed in the state and national constitutions, in the PRI party statutes, and in public declarations) and prevailing political practices (where a poorly integrated local elite rules with the tacit assent of the electorate).[3]

Finally, in evaluating this community as a political subsystem it is important to remember that our classification would probably change if we were to place Saragosa within the framework of regional politics. In that case there would be good reason to change the regime classification from Oligarchy to Guided Democracy, for one probably would find a higher sense of electoral potency. Likewise, since the local PAN was not able to present a challenge within the framework of community politics, but did operate within national elections and was moving in the direction of offering the PRI real competition in the Saragosa electoral district, a case could be made for defining political leadership within the district as Competitive Elite. In the last analysis, however, because of the unavailability of electoral statistics for Saragosa this question remains open to conjecture.

There is, however, one essential fact which remains constant and must not be overlooked. The major findings of this study suggest that in the analysis of local government in Mexico—and by extension, in much of Latin America—we have been asking the wrong questions. The crucial questions revolve not around the degree of

2. *Ibid.*, p. 82.
3. Because of the high degree of formalism in Saragosa politics, another way of examining this community would be to submit it to analysis by use of Riggs' prismatic model. In this instance we would find a transitional political subsystem fulfilling many of the relationships hypothesized in the prismatic model. See Fred W. Riggs, *Administration in Developing Countries: The Theory of Prismatic Society.*

local autonomy or local initiative, but around the communications and mobility networks integrating the community with state and national political systems. The effectiveness of local government in the setting of a centralized state, as is the case of Mexico, must be evaluated in terms of its responsiveness to local demands and necessities and the communication of these interests to state and national organizations. It is the responsiveness of such organizations which determines the effectiveness of the networks binding together local communities—hence the effectiveness of local governmental arrangements. The integrating mechanism for this system remains the PRI. The failings of local government in the specific instance of Saragosa stemmed not from the lack of local autonomy, but from a breakdown in the brokerage function provided by the local political leadership and the problem of readjusting that brokerage function to changing demands within the community.

APPENDIXES

A FURTHER NOTE ON METHODOLOGY

Regardless of Ward's admonition that the researcher working abroad may find it necessary to make the interview schedule "so flexible, so open-ended, and so tailored to each person being interviewed that the methods generally associated with survey research may not be appropriate" (Robert E. Ward *et al., Studying Politics Abroad: Field Research in the Developing Areas,* p. 105.), this project was conceptualized originally in terms of a structured interview guide based on a synthesis of the work of Robert Presthus in *Men at the Top* with a specific list of issues developed by Gladys M. Kammerer *et al.* in *The Urban Political Community.* This first questionnaire was not translated into Spanish until the researcher was in the field. Some two weeks were spent preparing a Spanish version with the assistance of associates in Saragosa. After initial experimentation with this questionnaire it was abandoned in favor of a more loosely structured one. This was the questionnaire used during the first five interviews. At the end of these interviews the researcher again revised it to make it more open-ended; this is the questionnaire published in Appendix II.

II
THE QUESTIONNAIRE

(The questionnaire is based on one used by Gladys M. Kammerer *et al.* in *The Urban Political Community.*)

A. Spanish

Introducción. Las preguntas que se formulan a continuación se refieren a diferentes aspectos del municipio de Saragosa y su cabecera. Este proyecto es lo que se llama un estudio de comunidad. Lo que me interesa saber es como funciona el municipio de Saragosa en sus aspectos económicos, sociales y políticos. Específicamente, tengo mucho interés en conocer el proceso por el cual los habitantes de Saragosa buscan soluciones a los problemas enfrentados por el municipio y su cabecera.

Quiero dejar claramente establecido que el proyecto que estoy realizando en Saragosa tiene fines puramente académicos. En consecuencia, todas las respuestas serán consideradas confidenciales y cualquier dato contenido en esta información será empleado de una manera anónima. El nombre del municipio, del mismo modo, quedará anónimo.

I. En su opinión, ¿cuáles son los problemas más importantes encarados por el municipio de Saragosa en los últimos treinta años? (Si el entrevistado ha vivido en Saragosa menos tiempo que el período mencionado, anote cuantos años ha vivido aquí y aplique la pregunta a este período.)

II. ¿Cómo ha cambiado la cuidad en lo económico, lo social y lo político durante los últimos treinta años — o durante el período que Ud. ha vivido aquí? (¿Población nueva? ¿ Industria nueva? ¿El tipo de persona que ocupa cargos públicos tales como Presidente municipal, Regidor o Síndico?)

III. Asuntos que han recibido atención recientemente. Esta parte del cuestionario incluye cinco temas específicos. Algunos de ellos le serán más conocídos que otros. Los temas incluídos son los siguientes: 1) la busca de industrias nuevas, 2) la construcción de la Presa ———, 3) la fijación de los precios agrícolas, 4) la supervivencia de la Facultad de Contabilidad y Administracíon de Empresas en Saragosa, y 5) la construcción del Bulevar ——— ——— (los protestos sobre su financiamiento.) (Sin duda, hay algunos temas que Ud. cree que son más importantes que otros. Por favor, comience con el que le parece más importante y termine con el que le parece menos importante.) Con respecto a cada tema, me interesan los aspectos siguientes:

1. ¿Quiénes están (estaban) interesados en el asunto? ¿Cuáles son (eran) los grupos interesados?
   a. ¿Hay algunas personas en particular que encabezan ese grupo? ¿Quiénes son? ¿Cuáles son sus ocupaciones?
   b. ¿Cuál es (era) su punto de vista sobre el asunto?
   c. ¿Hay (habían) otros grupos (personas) que han adoptado (adoptaron) un punto de vista determinado? ¿Quiénes son (eran)? ¿Cuáles son (eran) sus puntos de vista? ¿Hay (habían) otras relaciones entre estas personas (negocios, contactos sociales, etc.)?
2. ¿El Presidente municipal y/o el Ayuntamiento ha adoptado (adoptó) un punto de vista determinado?
   a. ¿Cuál es (era) este punto de vista?
   b. (Si tiene aplicación) ¿Quién era el Presidente municipal en aquel entonces?
3. En las resolución del asunto, ¿es (era) importante la actuación del Presidente municipal? ¿Del Ayuntamiento? Si la respuesta es negativa ¿quiénes resuelven (resolvieron) el problema?

IV. Grupos.
   1. ¿Hay personas que siguen de cerca las acciones del Presidente municipal? ¿Del Ayuntamiento?
      a. ¿Quiénes son esas personas? ¿Cuáles son sus ocupaciones? ¿A qué grupos u organizaciones pertenecen ellas?
      b. ¿Con quién(es) trabaja(n) en la solución de los problemas locales?
   2. ¿Hay personas a quienes el Presidente municipal (el Ayuntamiento) casi nunca hacen caso? ¿Por qué?

V. Relaciones institucionales.
   1. ¿Qué rol juega el Presidente municipal en las decisiones sobre lo que hay que hacer en la ciudad?
   2. ¿Qué rol tiene el Presidente municipal en la administración municipal diaria?
   3. ¿Qué poder tiene el Presidente municipal para: a) hacer nombramientos para puestos administrativos municipales, y b) pedir dimisiones? ¿Consulta al Ayuntamiento?
   4. ¿Cómo se prepara el presupuesto municipal de cada año?
   5. ¿Cómo se decide quien va a ser el próximo candidato del PRI para la Presidencia municipal? ¿Cómo se hace el resto de su planilla?

VI. Estrutura.
   1. ¿Diría Ud. que hay una persona o un grupo que domina en la ciudad y en el municipio?
      a. Si dice que sí, ¿quién(es) es (son)?
      b. Si dice que no, entonces ¿cómo funciona el municipio?
   2. ¿Hay grupos en Saragosa que están interesados en casi todos los asuntos importantes en discusión?

64

a. ¿Quiénes son?
b. ¿Por lo general vencen?
3. Si dice que no con respecto a la segunda pregunta, ¿Quiénes son los grupos y personas que tienen interés en los diversos asuntos importantes para la ciudad? ¿Podría darme algunos ejemplos?
4. En su opinión, ¿es la resolución de un punto en disputa dependiente del grupo que tiene mas interés en ello? ¿Podría darme algunos ejemplos?

VII. ¿Hay otras personas con quien debería platicar?
[This question was omitted on a regular basis after the twentieth interview and was used afterwards only intermittently.]

B. English
Introduction. The following questions refer to different aspects of the municipality of Saragosa and its urban center. [The nearest equivalent of the *cabecera*, here translated as "urban center," in United States experience is the county seat.] This project is what is known as a community study. What I am interested in is how the municipality functions in its economic, social, and political aspects. Specifically, I am very much interested in becoming familiar with the process by which the inhabitants of Saragosa look for solutions to the problems facing the municipality and its urban center.

I want to make it very clear that this project which I am carrying out in Saragosa is purely academic in nature. Consequently, all answers will be considered confidential and any facts taken from this material will be used anonymously. The name of the municipality, likewise, will remain anonymous.

I. In your opinion, what have been the most important problems facing the municipality of Saragosa during the last thirty years? (If the interviewee has lived in Saragosa less time, record how many years he has lived here and apply the question to this period.)

II. In what ways has the city changed over the last thirty years (or during the period you have lived here) in its economic, social, and political aspects? (New population? New industry? Same kinds of people occupying positions such as mayor, council members, and *síndico*?)

III. Matters which have received attention recently. This part of the questionnaire includes five "topics" in particular. [A suitable term for "issue" in Spanish could not be located. I did experiment with the term "problem" (or *problema*) but there was a general reluctance to speak of problems facing the city in such specific terms. The general answer I got when I referred to these five issues as problems was that they were not problems and as such there were no issues facing the city. Yet, with a slight switch in terminology to *asuntos* and *temas* I was able to avoid putting many interviewees on the defensive and draw out information on these topics.] Some of these topics will be better known to you than others. The topics I am referring to are the following: 1) the search for new industry, 2) the construction of the ——— Dam, 3) the setting of prices for agricultural products, 4) the survival of the School of Business Administration and Accounting in Saragosa, and 5) the construction of the ——— Boulevard (the protests over the way in which it was financed). (Without a doubt, there are some topics which you feel are more important than others. Please begin with the one that seems most important to you and end with the one that you feel is least important.) In each case, the following aspects interest me:

1. Who are (were) interested in the matter? What groups are (were) interested?
    a. Are there any persons in particular leading this group? Who are they? What are their occupations?
    b. What is (was) their stand on the matter?
    c. Are (were) there other groups (individuals) who have taken (took) a particular stand? Who are (were) they? What are (were) their stands? Are (were) there other points of contact between these individuals (business, social contacts, etc.)?
2. Have (Had) the mayor and the council taken a stand?
    a. What is (was) this stand?
    b. (If this is applicable) Who was the mayor at the time?
3. In resolving the matter, is (was) the participation of the mayor important? What about the council? If the reply is negative, who resolves(d) the problem?
IV. Groups. [The results of this section of the questionnaire were null.]
    1. Are there persons who follow closely the actions of the mayor? Of the council?
        a. Who are these people? What are their occupations? To what groups or organizations do they belong?
        b. With whom do they work for the resolution of local problems?
    2. Are there persons whom the mayor (the council) almost never listen to? Why?
V. Institutional relations.
    1. What is the role of the mayor in deciding what needs to be done in the city?
    2. What is the role of the mayor in day-to-day administration?
    3. What power does the mayor have in a) appointing persons to administrative positions in the municipality and b) in firing municipal employees? Does he consult the council?
    4. How is the budget prepared?
    5. How is it decided who will be the PRI's next candidate for mayor? How is the remainder of this slate selected?
VI. Structure.
    1. Would you say that there is any one person or group that runs the city?
        a. If the answer is yes, who is he (are they)?
        b. If the answer is no, how does the municipality function then?
    2. Are there groups in Saragosa who are interested in almost all the important matters which are discussed?
        a. Who are they?
        b. Do they usually win?
    3. If the answer to the second question is no, then who are the groups and persons that take interest in the different important matters facing the city? Could you give me some examples?
    4. In your opinion, is the resolution of a point in conflict dependent on the group that is most interested in it? Could you give me some examples?
    5. Are there other persons with whom I ought to talk (concerning these matters)?
        [This question was omitted on a regular basis after the twentieth interview and was used afterward only intermittently.]

III

A Check List of Issues

(These issues are based on those suggested by Kammerer *et al.* in *The Urban Politicial Community.*)

A. Spanish
  Aquí tiene Ud. algunos de los puntos en disputa que varias ciudades han encarado en los últimos veinte años. ¿Han sido de importancia en Saragosa?
  1. Industralización.
  2. Vivienda popular.
  3. Urbanización y obras públicas en la ciudad (abastecimiento de agua, agua potable, drenaje, electricidad, salud pública, alumbrado de las calles, pavimiento).
  4. Nuevas fuentes de ingresos para la municipalidad.
  5. Mano de obra.
  6. Precios de productos agrícolas
  7. El mejoramiento de las vías de comunicación: carretera, ferrocarril, aeropuerto.
  8. Problemas escolares (primario, secundario, superior).
  9. Obras públicas en el distrito: por ejemplo, campañas para mejorar la salud, obras hidráulicas.
  10. Conflictos políticos: el PRI v. otros.
  11. La forma de gobierno municipal.
  Considerando los diversos temas en la lista, ¿cuáles, diría Ud., han sido los cinco temas de más importancia?

B. English
  The following consists of a list of some of the issues that other cities have faced over the last twenty years. Have they been of importance in Saragosa?
  1. Industrialization.
  2. Public housing.
  3. Urbanization and public works in the city (water supply, drinking water, drainage, electricity, public health, street lighting, pavement).
  4. New sources of income for the municipality.
  5. Labor.
  6. The price of agricultural products.
  7. The improvement of communications: highway, railroad, airport.
  8. School problems (primary, secondary, advanced studies).
  9. Public works in the area: for example, campaigns to improve health, water supply (irrigation, dam construction, etc.).
  10. Politicial conflicts: the PRI v. others.
  11. The form of local government.
  Considering the various topics on this list, which, would you say, have been the five most important issues?

IV

This information is based on existing municipal records. Because of their incompleteness and the disorder of the municipal archives, it was not always possible to reconstruct each municipal council in its entirety. In the facing chart the first position in each case is that of the mayor. Numbers refer to individuals holding office more than once; "x's" to those who served only one term. Parentheses are used to indicate interruptions in the normal term of office by intervention from the state capital.

Over the twenty-nine-year period recorded above, twelve persons served on the municipal council twice, three served three times, and one served four. Numbers 8, 10, 13, and 14 cut across the factional divisions reported in the interviews. In two cases, 10 and 14, these men were peripheral to town politics. Number 13 was a labor union leader who by 1964 had aged considerably. He held his position primarily because of the need to balance representation and did not intervene actively in the local decision-making process. Number 8, however, cannot be dismissed so easily. As a former mayor and prominent local businessman, he had retained his influence across the years. During the summer of 1966 he was cited repeatedly as a local influential, but there was not enough interview data available to explain the nature of his participation. This was complicated by his unwillingness to discuss recent politics.

YEAR	1938	(1938)	(1939)a	1940	1942	1944	1946	(1946)b
COUNCIL		3	2-1		6	8	7	
MEMBERS	x 1 2 x 3 4 x x 5 x	(No change in council)	(No change in council)	x 6 x 7 x 4 x 14 x x	8 9 x 4 x x x x x	x 7 x x x x 10 x x x	x x 9 x x x x x x x x	x 11 x x 5
FACTION			1		Verde	Verde	Verde/Rojo	

YEAR	(1946)	1948	1950	1952	1955	1958	1961	1964
COUNCIL	7					15	16	
MEMBERS	12 (other positions not known)	x 13 x x x x x x 14 x x	x 11 x x x x x x x x x	x x 12 x 10 x x x	x x x x 15 x x x x x x	x x 16 13 x x x x x 8	x x x x x x x x x x	x x x x x x x x x x
FACTION	Rojo	Rojo	Rojo	Rojo	Rojo	Rojo	Rojo/Verde	Verde

aThis indicates two consecutive changes in the mayor.
bLasted only 6 days: February 2, 1946 to February 8, 1946.

BIBLIOGRAPHY

Adams, Richard N. "The Community in Latin America: A Changing Myth," *The Centennial Review*, VI (Summer, 1962), 409-34.
———. "Introduction" (to Social Organization) in Richard N. Adams, and Dwight B. Heath (eds.), *Contemporary Cultures and Societies of Latin America*. New York: Random House, 1965.
Agger, Robert E., Daniel Goldrich, and Bert E. Swanson. *The Rulers and the Ruled: Political Power and Impotence in American Communities*. New York: John Wiley and Sons, 1964.
Alisky, Marvin. "Mexico's Special Districts: Municipal Civic Betterment Boards," *Public Affairs Bulletin* (Arizona State University), IV (1965).
Anton, Thomas J. "Power, Pluralism, and Local Politics," *Administrative Science Quarterly*, VII (March, 1963), 425-57.
Bachrach, Peter, and Morton S. Baratz. "Decisions and Non-decisions: An Analytical Framework," *American Political Science Review*, LVII (September, 1963), 632-42.
———. "Two Faces of Power," *American Political Science Review*, LVI (December, 1962), 947-52.
Banco Nacional Hipotecario Urbano y de Obras Públicas, S.A. *Obras y Servicios Públicos*. México, D.F.: Banco Nacional Hipotecario Urbano y de Obras Públicas, 1959.
Banfield, Edward C., and James Q. Wilson. *City Politics*. New York: Vintage Books, Random House, 1966.
Bonjean, Charles M., and David M. Olson. "Community Leadership: Directions of Research," *Administrative Science Quarterly*, IX (December, 1964), 278-300.
Brand, Donald D. *Quiroga: A Mexican Municipio*. Washington, D.C.: Smithsonian Institution, 1951.
Brandenburg, Frank R. *The Making of Modern Mexico*. Englewood Cliffs, N.J.: Prentice-Hall, 1964.
Cline, Howard F. "Mexican Community Studies," *Hispanic American Historical Review*, XXXII (May, 1952), 212-42.
Comisión Nacional de los Salarios Mínimos. *Salarios Mínimos por Zonas y Municipios, 1964-1965*. Mexico, D.F., 1964.
Dahl, Robert A. *Who Governs? Democracy and Power in an American City*. New Haven, Conn.: Yale University Press, 1961.
Daland, Robert T. *A Strategy for Research in Comparative Urban Administration*. Bloomington, Ind.: Comparative Administrative Group, 1966.
D'Antonio, William V., and William H. Form. *Influentials in Two Border Cities: A Study in Community Decision-Making*. Notre Dame, Ind.: University of Notre Dame, 1965.
———, and Richard Suter. "Primary Elections in a Mexican Municipio: New Trends in Mexico's Struggle Toward Democracy." (Unpublished manuscript, mimeographed.)
———, William H. Form, Charles P. Loomis, and Eugene C. Erickson. "Institutional and Occupational Representation in Eleven Community Influence Systems," *American Sociological Review*, XXVI (June, 1961), 440-46.
Form, William H., and William V. D'Antonio. "Integration and Cleavage

BIBLIOGRAPHY

Among Community Influentials in Two Border Cities," *American Sociological Review*, XXIV (December, 1959), 804-14.

Hunter, Floyd. *Community Power Structure*. Chapel Hill, N.C.: University of North Carolina Press, 1953.

Janowitz, Morris (ed.). *Community Political Systems*. Glencoe, Ill.: The Free Press, 1961.

Kammerer, Gladys M., Charles D. Farris, John M. DeGrove, and Alfred B. Clubok. *The Urban Political Community: Profiles in Town Politics*. Boston: Houghton Mifflin Company, 1963.

Klapp, Orrin E., and L. Vincent Padgett. "Power Structure and Decision-Making in a Mexican Border City," *American Journal of Sociology*, LXV (January, 1960), 400-406.

Leeds, Anthony. "Brazilian Careers and Social Structure: A Case History and Model," in Richard N. Adams, and Dwight B. Heath (eds.), *Contemporary Cultures and Societies of Latin America*. New York: Random House, 1965.

Lerner, Daniel. *The Passing of Traditional Society: Modernizing the Middle East*. Glencoe, Ill.: The Free Press, 1963.

Lewis, Oscar. *Life in a Mexican Village: Tepoztlán Restudied*. Urbana, Ill.: The University of Illinois Press, 1963.

McQuown, Ruth, William R. Hamilton, and Michael P. Schneider. *The Political Restructuring of a Community*. Gainesville, Fla.: Public Administration Clearing Service, University of Florida, 1964.

México, Dirección General de Estadística. *Localidades del país con Población de 5000 y más Habitantes: Censo de 1960*. México, D.F., 1960.

————. *VIII Censo General de Población, 1960*. México, D.F., 1963

————. *VII Censo General de Población, 1950*. México, D.F., 1952.

————. *VI Censo de Población, 1940*. México, D.F., 1947.

————. *V Censo de Población, 15 de Mayo de 1930*. México, D.F., 1935.

México, Departamento de la Estadística Nacional. *Resumen del Censo General de Habitantes de 30 de Noviembre de 1921*. México, D.F., 1928.

Miller, Delbert C. "Democracy and Decision-Making in the Community Power Structure," in William V. D'Antonio and Howard J. Ehrlich (eds.), *Power and Democracy in America*. Notre Dame, Ind.: University of Notre Dame Press, 1961.

Padgett, L. Vincent. *The Mexican Political System*. Boston, Mass.: Houghton Mifflin, Co., 1966.

Presthus, Robert. *Men at the Top: A Study in Community Power*. New York: Oxford University Press, 1964.

Riggs, Fred W. *Administration in Developing Countries: The Theory of Prismatic Society*. Boston, Mass.: Houghton Mifflin Co., 1964.

————. Remarks at the Comparative Administration Group Conference. College Park, Md., April, 1966.

Scott, Robert E. *Mexican Government in Transition*. Urbana, Ill.: The University of Illinois Press, 1964.

————. "Mexico: The Established Revolution," in Lucian W. Pye, and Sidney Verba (eds.), *Political Culture and Political Development*. Princeton, N.J.: Princeton University Press, 1965.

Wagley, Charles, and Marvin Harris. "A Typology of Latin American Subcultures," in Richard N. Adams, and Dwight B. Heath (eds.), *Contemporary Cultures and Societies of Latin America*. New York: Random House, 1965.

Ward, Robert E., et al. *Studying Politics Abroad: Field Research in the Developing Areas*. Boston, Mass.: Little, Brown and Co., 1964.

72

Wheaton, William L. C. "Integration at the Urban Level: Political Influence and the Decision Process," in Philip E. Jacob and James V. Toscano (eds.), *The Integration of Political Communities*. Philadelphia, Pa.: J. B. Lippincott Company, 1964.

Wildavsky, Aaron. *Leadership in a Small Town*. Totowa, N.J.: Bedminster Press, 1964.

Williams, Oliver. "A Typology for Comparative Local Government," *Midwest Journal of Political Science* (May, 1961), 150-64.

Wolf, Eric R. "Aspects of Group Relations in a Complex Society: Mexico," in Richard N. Adams, and Dwight B. Heath (eds.), *Contemporary Cultures and Societies of Latin America*. New York: Random House, 1965.

UNIVERSITY OF FLORIDA MONOGRAPHS

Social Sciences

UNIVERSITY OF FLORIDA MONOGRAPHS

Social Sciences

13. *City Managers in Politics: An Analysis of Manager Tenure and Termination,* by G. M. Kammerer, C. D. Farris, J. M. DeGrove, and A. B. Clubok
14. *Recent Southern Economic Development as Revealed by the Changing Structure of Employment,* by E. S. Dunn, Jr.
15. *Sea Power and Chilean Independence,* by D. E. Worcester
16. *The Sherman Antitrust Act and Foreign Trade,* by A. Simmons
17. *The Origins of Hamilton's Fiscal Policies,* by D. F. Swanson
18. *Criminal Asylum in Anglo-Saxon Law,* by C. H. Riggs, Jr.
19. *Colonia Barón Hirsch, A Jewish Agricultural Colony in Argentina,* by M. D. Winsberg
20. *Time Deposits in Present-day Commercial Banking,* by L. L. Crum
21. *The Eastern Greenland Case in Historical Perspective,* by O. Svarlien
22. *Jacksonian Democracy and the Historians,* by A. A. Cave
23. *The Rise of the American Chemistry Profession, 1850-1900,* by E. H. Beardsley
24. *Aymara Communities and the Bolivian Agrarian Reform,* by W. E. Carter
25. *Conservatives in the Progressive Era: The Taft Republicans of 1912,* by N. M. Wilensky
26. *The Anglo-Norwegian Fisheries Case of 1951 and the Changing Law of the Territorial Sea,* by T. Kobayashi
27. *The Liquidity Structure of Firms and Monetary Economics,* by W. J. Frazer, Jr.
28. *Russo-Persian Commercial Relations, 1828-1914,* by M. L. Entner
29. *The Imperial Policy of Sir Robert Borden,* by H. A. Wilson
30. *The Association of Income and Educational Achievement,* by R. L. Lassiter, Jr.
31. *The Relation of the People to the Land in Southern Iraq,* by F. Baali
32. *The Price Theory of Value in Public Finance,* by D. R. Escarraz
33. *The Process of Rural Development in Latin America,* by T. Lynn Smith
34. *To Be or Not to Be . . . Existential-Psychological Perspectives on the Self,* edited by Sidney M. Jourard
35. *Politics in a Mexican Community,* by Lawrence S. Graham

Date Due
